the RUBBLE and the WALL

Sharing God's Heart to Restore What's Broken

BOOK 3 OF THE **HEARTWORK SERIES**

the RUBBLE and the WALL

Sharing God's Heart to Restore What's Broken

MIKE AND KELSEY DOMENY

To the King of our hearts, Jesus Christ. You don't need us,
but choose to involve us in Your Kingdom-building work.
May You make much of Yourself through this book.

To you, whose heart breaks for what breaks God's.
May your heart be ever-increasingly more aligned to His as
you dare to take your next steps.

Contents

A Note from the Authors

This book, *The Rubble and the Wall*, was originally published as *Next Best Yes* in 2024. It was anticipated to be the first of a series of three. Since then, we have leaned into God's changes of plans both personally and professionally, where we can now proudly present the Heartwork Series, and this, book three: *The Rubble and the Wall*.

If you read *Next Best Yes*, you will find much of the content here unchanged, but we have freshened and re-centered the conversation. We have removed some stories while adding new ones, and leaned more into letting the story of Nehemiah offer a path for you to follow. As always, we want God's Word to illuminate your steps, and we believe these changes have accomplished that.

While this book is presented as the finale of the Heartwork Series, we understand different readers will find themselves in different phases of God's work in their lives. If you feel like God is nudging you to take a scary step, even if it doesn't make sense, you're in the right place.

Thank you for reading.

Mike and Kelsey

Chapter One

The Prophet to Procrastinators

What a mess! Unbelievable. No one thought it would be this bad. For the first time in about seventy years, the Jews were finally standing in their homeland—their Promised Land—after being dragged out by the invading Babylonians. Only an aged handful would have remembered the glory of Jerusalem before the exile, before it was utterly ransacked. The wall, the gates, the homes, the pools, the markets, the temple—oh, the temple. Solomon's temple was erected at the height of Israel's power and world prestige. People came from distant countries to witness the glory that accompanies God's favor.

But now, God's people returned from distant lands to find God's city in shambles. They were sent home by the King of Persia, the bigger fish that subdued Israel's original captors. Though the Jews had their freedom, they had no home.

A large contingent of Jews, led by a man named Zerubbabel, began the arduous process of rebuilding their city. Over time, Jerusalem was once again filled with cute little homes with rooftop gardens, bustling marketplaces, and social baths.

"What about the temple?" people would ask periodically. But the question was always met with sighs and eye rolls.

"It's not the right time."

I mean, this is *the temple* we're talking about. It's one thing to rebuild old man Zadok's one-bedroom, flat-topped farmhouse. It's an entirely different project to rebuild the physical representation of God's presence among His people! It was built by *Solomon, the son of David,* for goodness sake! He had every resource, tool, and artisan at his fingertips. But now? We have a pile of rubble and dirt under our fingernails.

"Not now. We can't properly honor God with what we have now."

"We'll build the temple later. When it makes sense."

The citizenry would reach a consensus, shrug, and straighten their wall hangings. Besides, life wasn't quite back to "normal" yet.

"It's not the right time," they'd repeat to each other.

They were in a drought, the economy was fragile, and life was still hard. The big project would be best suited for when there was abundance and excess. The best course of action would be to make the best of the situation, be glad they had a home, and cross that bridge when they get there.

A knock sounded on Zerubbabel's door. "Governor?"

"Come in." Zerubbabel looked up to see Haggai, an older man whose wisdom Zerubbabel had come to appreciate in rebuilding the city. "Haggai! Come, have a seat. I was just considering what it would take to install a gate in the back courtyard of the governor's house. Tell me what you think—"

"Zerubbabel... the Lord sent me to tell you something."

"The Lord—oh! Goodness, yes, of course," Zerubbabel cleared the tabletop. "Please, tell me."

"This is what the Lord of Heaven's Armies says: 'The people are saying, "The time has not yet come to rebuild the house of the Lord." Why are you living in luxurious houses while my house lies in ruins?'" (Haggai 1:2,4).

Zerubbabel's face dropped. "The time has not yet come" was one of his go-to replies. Apparently, he was not on the same page as God. He glanced up at the crown molding above his cabinets. For the first time, it brought him no satisfaction.

Haggai continued, "This is what the Lord of Heaven's Armies says: 'Look at what's happening to you! You have planted much but harvest little. You eat but are not satisfied. You drink but are still thirsty. You put on clothes but cannot keep warm. Your wages disappear as though you were putting them in pockets filled with holes! Look at what's happening to you!'"

Zerubbabel had nothing to say. The Lord's words through Haggai pretty much summed it up.

"'Now go up into the hills, bring down timber, and rebuild my house. Then I will take pleasure in it and be honored,' says the Lord. 'You hoped for rich harvests, but they were poor. And when you brought your harvest home, I blew it away. Why? Because my house lies in ruins,' says the Lord of Heaven's Armies, 'while all of you are busy building your own fine houses'" (Haggai 1:5-9).

Look at what's happening

Are you in a painfully similar situation to the Jews in this story? You see a gaping hole in your life or the world around you where God's presence should be. Maybe His presence used to be there, but it got destroyed or neglected. You feel like you *should* do something about it—build it, repair it, create it—but it's too big a project for now. Maybe later, when you have more money, more time, more people around, more clarity and understanding of what it should be. Instead, you sigh and shrug.

"The time has not yet come," you say (or something like that), and you return to your routine. You show up to the office or perhaps do some work around the house. Life isn't exactly abundant, but it's what makes sense, and it's what you can handle right now.

The Lord challenges you, like He challenged Zerubbabel and the Jews, to "look at what's happening to you." If you're being honest, you may feel like you are putting food on the table but are not satisfied with how life is going. You're working overtime to make more money, but more money only seems to lead to more expensive problems. You hoped for a better life by now, and maybe you've been able to upgrade some aspects of it, but your efforts ultimately feel pointless. You have a choice. You can either prioritize building God's Kingdom or your "thingdom."

> **YOU CAN EITHER PRIORITIZE GOD'S KINGDOM OR YOUR "THINGDOM."**

Right now, God's house lies in ruins. I (Mike) don't know what project God's house represents in your life, but God wants to take up residence somewhere—in your life and others', in your neighborhood and those across the world, among the bodies of believers and in the hearts of unbelievers, and at your workplace and in your family. No matter how much attention you give to your own work and life, you can't escape the nagging feeling that one or more of those areas desperately needs God's presence. You probably have an idea of what you could build or do to give God the glory and the victory, but it feels impossible. It's easy to put it off and prioritize other things. It's easy to procrastinate.

Procrastination isn't laziness. Procrastination is a response to feeling as if we have a lack of clarity or resources. Think about what you're procrastinating on right now. I bet you're not lazy. My guess is you aren't sure exactly what the next step is. You feel like you don't know how to do something or don't have what you need to do it.

It may sound simplistic, but take note of God's push to Zerubbabel. "Go up into the hills, bring down timber, and rebuild my house."

He's effectively saying, "Go where I tell you, use the available resources, and start what you know you need to do."

God swept away every crutch the procrastinator could lean on.

I don't know how to start!
... "Leave your routine and go where I tell you."
I don't have enough time or resources!
... "The time is now, and you have what you need."
I don't know what exactly I'm supposed to do!
... "Build my Kingdom."

Is it really that simple? For now, yes. Of course, the temple would require more than wood from the hills. More steps are involved beyond bringing down timber. But yes. *Obedient actions are the cycle-breaking difference-makers that move you closer to the fulfilling Kingdom-building life God desires for you.*

Where we're headed

For the rest of this book, we'll continue looking at God's work with His people as they rebuilt Jerusalem. Nehemiah will enter the picture, and his story will provide the framework for our conversation. We'll also introduce you to some Kingdom-seeking Jesus followers like you, whose stories will encourage you in your own Kingdom work. Through it all, you will learn how to share God's heart for what is broken, and recognize your unique role in God's work.

I'd also like to bring your attention to some additional opportunities to discuss and reflect throughout this conversation. In the back of the book, you'll find appendices that correspond to each chapter. There, you'll find questions, guides, and additional content to turn this "quick read" into a traveling companion. Of course, the best companions are the people around you, so invite some friends to read and discuss with you along the way!

But before we go further, we'd like to take a moment to invite you to pray. Every step of pursuing God's plan for your life must be smothered in prayer. We'll share our prayer for you; we hope you'll pray it with us. After that, put this book down. Really! Close it. Nothing we have to say compares to what your Heavenly Father can speak into your heart. Start with Him, then come back here and we'll start our journey with the story of Nehemiah.

> *Father God, You are everything that matters. We fall short of Your glory, but You delight in forgiving us when we ask. Please show us where our hearts have been far from You and give us the humility to repent. We pray for our friend reading this now. Align our hearts to Yours, make our hearts break for what breaks Your heart, and make us discontent with any life that is not fully submitted to You. Then, fill us with the courage to say "yes" to follow where You lead, even if it's scary. Amen.*

See Appendix A for some introductory questions, great for personal reflection as you start on this journey, or for an opening discussion among friends.

Chapter Two

The Heart-Breaking Problem

Fast forward from where we last left God's people in Jerusalem. Zerubbabel led them to rebuild the temple slowly but surely. Frankly, it wasn't as magnificent as the previous temple, but God was more concerned with the heart driving the effort. With that, He was pleased. God's glory filled the city, and Jerusalem was starting to look like its former self.

Not all of the Jewish exiles hurried to Jerusalem the first chance they got. Even after King Cyrus released them from the Babylonian-turned-Persian kingdom, many stayed. After all, over seventy years of exile, entire generations were born and raised in the kingdom. They didn't know any different, and some had developed comfortable lives.

Nehemiah was one such Jewish resident of Persia. He lived and worked with diligence and integrity to the point that he served in the king's palace as his cupbearer.

The book of Nehemiah begins like an epic film. Visualize the establishing shots of lush rivers and plateaus. From the horizon rises the fortress of Susa, a palace built to intimidate. A crisp autumn breeze blows brown and orange leaves through the air and across a dirt path. Sandaled feet step into frame, and the dried leaves crunch beneath the weight of the wearer. Whoever these people are and wherever they're going, they move with purpose. The camera follows the back of the heads of men who knock and then enter a large room.

The occupant of the room speaks. "Hanani! Tell me the news." He senses the report is not good, and so he presses. "Please, speak."

The marching men stare at each other, unsure how to describe what they saw. The one we now know as Hanani speaks up.

"Nehemiah, my brother, things are not going well for those who returned to the province of Judah. They are in great trouble and disgrace." Nehemiah's face distorts with grief. Hanani delivers the harsh truth, "the wall of Jerusalem has been torn down."

"Even the gates?" a distraught Nehemiah pleads, grasping for any hope left.

Hanani hesitates to respond, but forces out the words, "Destroyed by fire."

Nehemiah crumples to the floor and weeps.

It's not just a wall

Nehemiah's response may seem extreme to modern residents of un-walled cities, but in his day, a city's wall was crucial to its safety and honor. Without a wall, anything from rabid dogs to enemy troops could walk into town and take whatever they wanted. Beyond physical protection, a walled city meant an honored city. Jerusalem was the home of the physical representation of God's presence, the temple. God didn't need a wall to protect His home or His people (Jerusalem was only conquered in the first place because it was part of their punishment for dishonoring God and His law for so long). A wall around God's city showcased a sense of honor among the surrounding nations. "The God of Israel is holy, and we should approach Him with reverence."

A pile of rubble communicated the opposite. "Walk in here and trample us again if you want. There's nothing special about Israel or its God."

That's what broke Nehemiah's heart. It was not about a pile of rocks. It was what the mess represented: neglect, dishonor, and mundanity. None of those traits were befitting of God and His chosen nation.

You don't need to be an emotional person to reach the point Nehemiah did. Tears are not the sole indicator that your heart breaks for a problem. Mike hardly ever cries; I (Kelsey) wept when I reached the end of a tin of lavender shortbread cookies.

Rather, you know your heart has broken because of a problem when you can't continue living the way you had before. Before recognizing the problem, you could go about your work just fine. You'd clock in. You'd wipe the coffee ring off your desk. You'd nod at Trevor from accounting on the way to the bathroom. You'd go home, spill a tiny bit of lasagna on your jeans, and call it a night.

But now, you think about the problem in the shower. Your thoughts drift toward it during the meeting. Your internet search history reveals you've been researching it. Maybe it has affected your emotions as it did Nehemiah. People who know you might express their concern that you look tired, distracted, or sad.

If any of this sounds familiar, you have a God-given recognition of a problem. Once you see a problem, you can't unsee it. You can't go on living life as you once did. Coming to this realization can be scary. Even scarier is the recognition that you may be required to do something about it.

Where love comes in

"Fall in love with the problem, not the solution." This often-quoted piece of entrepreneurial advice was made mainstream when Uri Levine, founder of the GPS navigation app Waze, made it the title of his book. The concept acknowledges and stands in contrast to the fact that we tend to fall in love with our *solution* to a problem—our project, our product, or our service. But what happens when the culture, technology, or even God takes an unexpected turn, and our solution doesn't serve people as well as it once did? If you love your solution of offering movies for people to take home and watch, what happens when it becomes possible to have them delivered or, better yet, streamed from home? Sorry, Blockbuster.

Continuing that example, let's say, however, you identify the problem: People don't have convenient access to movies and entertainment without going to a theater. If you fall in love with that problem, you'll do whatever it takes to make it easy for people to access what they want.

Hopefully, your heart is bent toward a more Kingdom-centered problem, but the example still serves to show that solutions come and go, but problems persist until they're solved. Therefore, practitioners of Levine's advice would say, fall in love with the problem so you stay in the fight until the war is won.

There is wisdom in this, but it's not the complete picture. As followers of Jesus, we have a call beyond that. We want our hearts and minds to be grounded in Scripture, and when we hold the ideas of love and problems up to Scripture, God is clear about where our love should be focused, and it's not on problems. Deuteronomy 6:5 lays it out. "You must love the Lord your God with all your heart, all your soul, and all your strength."

When pressed to pick the most important commandment, Jesus gives the reprise of Deuteronomy in Matthew 22:37-39.

"Jesus replied, 'You must love the Lord your God with all your heart, all your soul, and all your mind.' This is the first and greatest commandment. A second is equally important: 'Love your neighbor as yourself.' "

Those close to him, upon hearing this answer, pushed Jesus to define what a "neighbor" is (so they could justify their racism and hypocrisy, presumably). So Jesus told a story. You've heard it. We call it the Parable of the Good Samaritan. You can refresh your memory in Luke 10 if you'd like.

In the story, a Jewish man had been beaten and left for dead. That's the problem. A couple influential Jews came along who decided it wasn't their problem, and they avoided him. Then another man approached—a man from Samaria, a region of people who for hundreds of years held mutual animosity against the Jews. Filled with surprising love and mercy, he found solutions and solved the man's problem. It cost him money, time, and reputation, but he was moved by love for another human being, and he did whatever was needed to solve the problem.

The heart of the story isn't what the Samaritan *did*. The heart of the story is *why* Jesus told it in the first place. Remember, Jesus was answering the question, "Who is my neighbor?"

Essentially, "Who do I have to love?"

His answer? Every human being is a neighbor, and we are called to love one another no matter our differences. The focus is on the person. Mike's favorite t-shirt sums up Jesus' words: "Love God. Love People."

Our love must be for God and for people. The more you love God, the more you'll love what God loves and weep over what breaks God's heart. Sure, there are problems in the world you could identify which, if you were to offer a solution, could generate plenty of income. You could recognize problems that would lead to fame and popularity if you got involved. You could jump on board with problems that are trending or clickable or would generate thousands of impressions on social media, but we pray you don't get sucked into solving profitable problems.

ALLOW GOD TO BREAK YOUR HEART FOR WHAT BREAKS HIS.

Instead, allow God to break your heart for what breaks His. Allow God's priorities to shape yours when it comes to what problem you are impassioned to solve. Then, you can be confident that the heartbreak you feel is a reflection of God's own heart for people. Jesus is eager to change and heal people, and a shared heart means Jesus is inviting you to share in His mission with His strength.

There are problems in the world—more than your heart can handle. Some are impossible for you to ignore, and you care deeply about them, but the *reason* you should care so deeply about the problems is because those problems affect *people*. Do not simply fall in love with problems. Like Nehemiah, care about what God cares about, love the people He loves, and then work with God to offer solutions to the problems His people face.

Ultimately, if we were to offer an edit to the popular "Fall in love with the problem" mantra, we'd say, "Love the *people* who *have* the problem."

Being moved

This book doesn't end here for a reason. It's not enough to simply recognize a problem. It's not even enough to have compassion for the people who are affected by the problem. Like Nehemiah, we must let compassion for people move us to action.

When Jesus approached Jerusalem's walls hundreds of years after Nehemiah rebuilt them, consider His emotions as He thought of the people in the city. "But as he came closer to Jerusalem and saw the city ahead, he began to weep. 'How I wish today that you, of all people, would understand the way to peace. But now it is too late, and peace is hidden from your eyes'" (Luke 19:41-42).

Jesus' heart broke, and He wept at the thought of all those people living without peace, but He didn't sit in His sadness. The heartbreak drove Him to action. By the end of the week, He would willingly subject Himself to being stretched out on a cross, beaten, mocked, and killed—all in the name of offering the solution the people truly needed: the Prince of Peace Himself.

Heartbreak, if acted upon, leads to breakthrough. Feeling the weight of the problem must lead to action. But your next step will be fruitless if it is taken in your own strength and understanding.

See Appendix B for some tough but important questions relating to the problem that breaks your heart and God's.

Chapter Three

The Heart-Bending Prayer

Nehemiah felt the comforting weight of his friends' hands on his back as his body shook with tears. Together, they felt their hearts break for the disgrace their people and their God must have been facing. They were sad, angry, and restless. They had to do something! But... what?

The one big problem was accompanied by several related problems: Would Nehemiah himself have to go to Jerusalem? What about his full-time job in service to the king of Persia? Would this look like abandonment or treason? How would he travel that long distance safely? How would he find enough materials to rebuild a city? How long would the project take? What would the locals think? What would the enemies think?

Beaten down by the weight of all that needed to happen to solve the problem, Nehemiah knew it was more than he could handle alone.

He could have forged ahead and faked it until he made it. He could have taken the time to strategize a 1-, 5-, and 10-year plan. Instead, he went to the One who put the problem on his heart in the first place. Nehemiah mourned, fasted, and prayed to God for days.

Planning to pray, praying to plan

People love Jeremiah 29:11. It is regularly emblazoned on mugs, t-shirts, and social media posts. If you're not a frequent Hobby Lobby shopper, allow us to jog your memory.

"'For I know the plans I have for you,' declares the Lord, 'plans to prosper you and not to harm you, plans to give you hope and a future'" (Jeremiah 29:11, NIV).

We get very excited about the prospering part. It's encouraging to know there's hope out there for us in our future. We think, "Yes! God's on my side!"

But consider how the sentence starts. "I know the plans *I have* for you."

He has plans for you. He did not say, "I know the plans you want for yourself, and I'll honor those to give you these things."

He said He knows the plans *He* has for you. Proverbs 16:9 puts it this way: "We can make our plans, but the Lord determines our steps."

The only way you can be successful in the plans the Lord has for you is if you take them to Him and let Him shape your plans.

Once you fall in love with the people who have the problem, you must realize you cannot actually solve the problem. God can. You can make plans to solve the problem, but they will fail if they are not aligned with His plans. He's the one that put the problem on your heart. He's the one who will solve it.

George Müller's heart broke for the innumerable orphans barely scraping by on the streets of 19th-century England. He opened the doors of his own home to care for a handful, but it soon became evident to him that he would need to build more than a few orphanages across the country.

Indeed, by the end of his life, he had founded 117 orphanages. Müller was not a wealthy philanthropist. He didn't lean on the expertise of a business partner. He was not a CEO with a lengthy track record of successful start-ups. Yet, he channeled a modern-day equivalent of over 100 million dollars to house, feed, educate, and equip over 10,000 orphans in his lifetime. It might surprise you, then, to hear Müller's plan to finance this massive orphan care network.

Prayer.

Prayer was the plan. Müller didn't embark on fundraising campaigns or hire sales teams. He didn't ask for even a small donation from the people he met. Every dollar (or pound, I suppose, in his case) was unsolicited, voluntarily donated by people who felt God's prompt to contribute to the work.

He reflected in his autobiography, "I also particularly longed to be used by God in getting the dear orphans trained up in the fear of God; but still, the first and primary object of the work was, and still is, that God might be magnified by the fact that the orphans under my care are provided with all they need, only *by prayer and faith*, without any one being asked by me or my fellow-laborers, whereby it may be seen that God is faithful still, and hears prayer still."[1]

George Müller's heart didn't break only for orphans. He recognized another problem: people had lost sight of the truth that God is faithful, and eager to answer prayers. God had a plan to address both problems at once, and Müller submitted to a plan of prayer that defied human sense.

Nehemiah's prayer

The way Nehemiah approached God in response to hearing the news about Jerusalem's fallen walls and burned gates teaches us how we ought to pray when our heart breaks for a problem. He starts this way:

Prayer Principle #1: Declare who God is.

"O Lord, God of heaven, the great and awesome God who keeps his covenant of unfailing love with those who love him and obey his commands, listen to my prayer! "(Neh. 1:5)

Whenever we approach God, we must acknowledge His majesty and power. Consider how Jesus taught His disciples to pray: He began, "Our Father in Heaven, Holy is Your Name."

Both Jesus and Nehemiah come to the throne first, declaring God's power, sovereignty, and holiness. Recognizing God's authority and goodness isn't for *His* benefit. He knows who He is and what He can do. No, *we* are the ones who need reminding of who He is. *We need to remind ourselves that prayer is not the answer to our problems—the One we're praying to is.*

If we rush into prayer with our needs, our hopes, our desires, and our worries at the forefront of the conversation, we miss an opportunity to rest. When we come into prayer, we first recognize to whom it is we speak, and we can rest right away in His presence. Regardless of the outcome of our prayers, we can access peace immediately. We can sit at His throne, knowing He already knows our needs (Matthew 6:32).

When we're with Him, we can experience the peace Paul talks about in Philippians 4:6-7. "Don't worry about anything; instead, pray about everything. Tell God what you need, and thank him for all he has done. Then, you will experience God's peace, which exceeds anything we can understand. His peace will guard your hearts and minds as you live in Christ Jesus."

By praying about everything and pausing to understand *who* is hearing our prayers, we can experience peace that doesn't make sense. We can know that He is with us; He has gone before us; He is just and quick to forgive, and we can trust Him with what troubles us.

So, Prayer Principle #1 is to tell God what you love about Him. This helps you experience peace in the midst of your problems by remembering who is actually in charge. In light of who *He* is, our second prayer principle will help us remember who *we* are.

Prayer Principle #2: Confess your own sin.

"Look down and see me praying night and day for your people Israel. I confess that we have sinned against you. Yes, even my own family and I have sinned! We have sinned terribly by not obeying the commands, decrees, and regulations that you gave us through your servant Moses" *(Neh. 1:6-7).*

After we take a good look at who God is, our immediate next move is to confess our sins and shortcomings. We see in Scripture when someone comes face-to-face with God's holiness, they can't help but declare their unworthiness. Isaiah had a vision of God on His throne surrounded by worshiping seraphim. His response is recorded in Isaiah 6:5.

"Then I said, 'It's all over! I am doomed, for I am a sinful man. I have filthy lips, and I live among a people with filthy lips. Yet I have seen the King, the Lord of Heaven's Armies.'"

When we pause to truly consider God's glory and majesty, our own shortcomings ought to be evident. And we must confess our sins. It's imperative to keep walking with the Lord. Nehemiah's confession was crucial if he wanted to continue the work and enter the promised land. His admittance of Israel's sin is echoed in Hebrews with a strong warning.

> That is why the Holy Spirit says, "Today when you hear his voice, don't harden your hearts as Israel did when they rebelled, when they tested me in the wilderness. There your ancestors tested and tried my patience, even though they saw my miracles for forty years. So I was angry with them, and I said, 'Their hearts always turn away from me. They refuse to do what I tell them.' So in my anger I took an oath: 'They will never enter my place of rest.'"

> Be careful then, dear brothers and sisters. Make sure that your own hearts are not evil and unbelieving, turning you away from the living God... So let us do our best to enter that rest. But if we disobey God, as the people of Israel did, we will fall (Hebrews 3:7-12, 4:11).

The people of Israel sinned, disobeyed God, hardened their hearts, and were unrepentant, and that's what got them into the mess with Jerusalem's walls being destroyed in the first place.

> And who was it who rebelled against God, even though they heard his voice? Wasn't it the people Moses led out of Egypt? And who made God angry for forty years? Wasn't it the people who sinned, whose corpses lay in the wilderness? And to whom was God speaking when he took an oath that they would never enter his rest? Wasn't it the people who disobeyed him? (Hebrews 3:16-18)

The sin of those who were led out of Egypt kept them from entering the promised land. Then Joshua led them to the promised land where they lived until they sinned with unrepentant hearts again, and God allowed the city to be captured and the people taken captive by Assyria and then Babylon. And now Nehemiah is here, on the heels of generations of sin as well as his personal and familial sin, seeing the shame of the people of Israel in a broken-down city. So, before he sets to work rebuilding the physical city, he gets to work rebuilding his spiritual health. He confesses sin and sets himself in the right frame of mind and heart to be used. Once again, it's not for God's benefit that we confess our sins, it's for ours.

God already knows everything. Nothing is hidden. Yet, our purpose, peace, and prosperity will be hidden from us if we do not repent of our sins. We must allow God's Word to infiltrate our hearts and do some surgery. It is alive, powerful, and sharper than a double-edged sword (see Hebrews 4:12-13).

We must be willing to take an honest look at ourselves in light of the standard of God's Word.

Confessing our shortcomings will make it harder for our enemy to cultivate pride in our hearts as we go about God's work. Confessing our sins and shortcomings once again puts God at the helm of this whole thing. It reminds us we aren't capable on our own, and any Kingdom-building we are about to do will only be done because of His will, His power, and His might. If you want to start what God put on your heart, get out of the way and humbly let Him lead you.

Prayer Principle #3: Lean on God's Promises.

"Please remember what you told your servant Moses: 'If you are unfaithful to me, I will scatter you among the nations. But if you return to me and obey my commands and live by them, then even if you are exiled to the ends of the earth, I will bring you back to the place I have chosen for my name to be honored'" (Neh. 1:8-9).

Notice how Nehemiah quotes God back to God. He draws strength for what he's about to do, knowing God already promised to do it long ago. He's recalling this promise from Deuteronomy.

In the future, when you experience all these blessings and curses I have listed for you, and when you are living among the nations to which the Lord your God has exiled you, take to heart all these instructions. If at that time you and your children return to the Lord your God, and if you obey with all your heart and all your soul all the commands I have given you today, then the Lord your God will restore your fortunes. He will have mercy on you and gather you back from all the nations where he has scattered you. Even though you are banished to the ends of the earth, the Lord your God will gather you from there and bring you back again. The Lord your God will return you to the land that belonged to your ancestors, and you will possess that land again. Then he will make you even more prosperous and numerous than your ancestors!

The Lord your God will change your heart and the hearts of all your descendants, so that you will love him with all your heart and soul and so you may live! (Deuteronomy 30:1-6)

God is not surprised when Nehemiah comes to Him. "In the future, when you experience all these blessings and curses," it begins.

That's where Nehemiah is! God knew where they would be and what they would be up against, and He gave them a plan for reconciliation. He formed an entire game plan. If you return to the Lord and obey (that's on you), then I will restore your fortune, gather you back together, and make you more prosperous than before (that's on Him). As a result, you will be restored to a loving relationship with God. (Amen!)

Nehemiah's recollection of God's promise in Deuteronomy shows us two things. (1) God already knew this was going to be a problem, and He had a plan to solve it. (2) We need to know God's promises.

What has God promised? We find plenty of promises in God's Word that apply to you and the work He's given you. Here are a few you can hold up, anchor your hopes in, and build your life on.

- *If you seek first the Kingdom and live righteously, God will provide all you need* (Matthew 6:25-33).

- *You will not be abandoned. What God starts, He finishes, and that includes the work in you* (Philippians 1:6).

- *God promises to hear you and be near to you when your heart is broken* (Psalm 34:17-19).

- *It's not all up to us. Even when we lose faith, God remains faithful* (2 Timothy 2:11-13).

These are just a few of the promises in God's Word to which we can anchor our hearts. In Appendix C, we've included even more. Please don't skim past these promises. In fact, I encourage you to pause this chapter for a moment, and read through them. Remind yourself who God is. Let God remind you who you are. Get on the same page as God. Let His promises wash over you before you lift another finger. Then come back and finish this chapter when you're ready.

Prayer Principle #4: Offer yourself as a servant.

"The people you rescued by your great power and strong hand are your servants. O Lord, please hear my prayer! Listen to the prayers of those of us who delight in honoring you" (Neh. 1:10-11a).

It sounds quite Christian to pray, "Please use me, God!" We've been in countless backstage prayer huddles with bands and speakers where this plea has been shot to heaven.

GOD DOESN'T NEED YOU.

While the heart behind it may be a willing one, it tends to neglect an important truth about God's work: God doesn't need you. If that's true, what are you asking? Are you asking Him to use you more than others? To pick you first for the volleyball team? To say you're more useful than someone else?

This is finely tuned heart surgery. If you sense a little friction here, take note of Nehemiah's prayer as he offers himself and his countrymen as God's servants. Simply because God gave you the idea doesn't mean He has to use you to do it.

Instead of praying "Use me," take the servant's posture and offer a prayer (with the heart to match), "I am your servant. I'm ready and willing, and I will celebrate you using anybody to do this work."

See the difference? Let the distinction settle into your heart as you move forward.

Prayer Principle #5: Ask for favor.

"Please grant me success today by making the king favorable to me. Put it into his heart to be kind to me" (Neh. 1:11b).

Nehemiah had a job as the cupbearer to the king. That is not a simple job that comes with unlimited paid time off. He knew he would have to talk to the king about his plans if he was going to have any chance of seeing his visions come to reality.

Often, the God-given work on our hearts will require difficult conversations to redefine our relationships with key people around us. Saying "yes" to God will almost guarantee you're going to say "no" to someone else, and that is always hard. But their support, whatever that looks like, is their part in the work. Remember, our previous Prayer Principle reminded us that God can use anyone He wants. The person you think is most in your way is there because they're part of God's plan for this thing happening.

So when you see hard conversations and big asks coming up, pray for favor. Pray, "God, please grant me favor in the eyes of those whose hearts need to be softened toward this work."

That prayer acknowledges God will get the glory for success, and it's not because you are clever or persuasive. It also opens the door for other people to experience the blessing and favor of God for being involved in this work. This prayer sees people as potential partners instead of obstacles.

Nehemiah understood the importance of keeping an open prayer channel with God throughout the process. In fact, his book records *fourteen* prayers—all at key moments before difficult interactions. You would do well to go to God before each step, each challenge, and each obstacle. Take to heart how Nehemiah offered his prayer.

1. Declare who God is.

2. Confess your sin.

3. Lean on God's promises.

4. Offer yourself as a servant.

5. Ask for favor with others.

Remember, the journey ahead is not primarily about wall building and rubble relocation. It's about your heart, growing your relationship with Jesus, and becoming who God wants you to be. It's about sharing God's heart in the midst of all the brokenness. Your heart aligns with His through prayer. If you skip prayers of humility like this, you're skipping the very essence of what God sees as success.

See Appendix C to help you form your own prayer similar to Nehemiah's prayer, and explore God's promises throughout the Bible.

Chapter Four

The Imperfect Step

Nehemiah was the king's cupbearer. That meant he was in a respected position in the royal court. He would hand-deliver libations to the king—in this case, King Artaxerxes. Plots against the royals were an ever-present threat, so the cupbearer had to be a servant of integrity. And in the event a drink was particularly suspicious, the cupbearer would taste it before serving it. If the cupbearer died, they knew the drink was poisoned. Basically, the cupbearer was a human buffer between ne'er-do-wells and the ruler they wished dead. Because the job was dangerous, it also paid well! If being poisoned was a daily occupational hazard, at least your family had a 401(k).

Nehemiah had a nice job. He had position, money, authority, and respect. However, after praying about the problem he saw in Jerusalem, Nehemiah couldn't keep living the way he had. Something had to change, and he knew he needed to take action. Have you ever been so consumed with your own thoughts that you forgot to check your face? That must have been the case for Nehemiah because the king noticed.

"Hey, Neo, you don't look so good" (this is loosely translated from the original Hebrew). For reasons previously mentioned, I'm sure the king was a bit unnerved to see his cupbearer looking out of sorts. "What's wrong?"

Oh no! Nehemiah wasn't trying to gain attention or sympathy. Servants of the king don't show up to the court with anything less than a cheerful attitude. Now, Nehemiah's face was less "I'm sad for my people" and more "I'm about to die if the king doesn't like the next words out of my mouth." He was honest, hoping his rapport with the king would save him, and told the king what was on his mind.

Nehemiah recounts, "Then I was terrified, but I replied, 'Long live the king! How can I not be sad? For the city where my ancestors are buried is in ruins, and the gates have been destroyed by fire'" (Neh. 2:3).

He had prayed for favor in this conversation. Whether or not God answered would become evident with the king's reply.

"How can I help?"

Nehemiah sighed in relief, prayed again, then courageously asked the king for all that had been floating around in his mind: Time off to go rebuild the city, letters for safe passage through the territories, and IOUs for the king's forest manager to secure lumber and supplies for rebuilding.

Remember, Nehemiah wasn't in the construction business. He wasn't a builder or an architect. He hadn't seen the damage for himself; he was going through all this trouble based on a verbal report. He didn't know the full extent of the problem nor everything that would be needed for a solution. But Nehemiah did know he needed to take action, even if it wasn't perfect and even if it didn't make complete sense.

"And the king granted these requests because the gracious hand of God was on me." (Nehemiah 2:8b)

Nehemiah quit his job and moved to a new country to begin work on a project he had no experience doing and had no way of knowing all the ways it would work out. He had supplies, but did he have too much? Not enough? Did he even have the right stuff? The point is it didn't matter. He took action based on what he knew and what he could do *now*.

My (Kelsey's) mom has a theory that what you play as a child is the kind of career you should pursue as an adult. When you were in your most uninhibited state of life before pressure and expectations and bills and retirement plans and accolades and paychecks came into play, what made you happy simply by doing it?

Some of my earliest memories are of setting up two kitchen chairs in the foyer of our suburban Michigan split-level home. These two seats were reserved for my parents. The staircase was a massive waterfall surrounded by cliffs and forests of pillows. My cast was made up of a stuffed bear, a stuffed dog, and a fluffy friend my brother called "Bear Dog" because he wasn't sure which one it was. I was the director, choreographer, and lead actor of a tragic but heroic tale of slippery slopes and holding on for dear life. I have loved theatre from the moment I could pretend, and so, with my mom's encouragement, I declared a theatre major when I went off to college.

While I was enacting an epic drama of Tennessee Williams proportions, Leigha was a young girl thousands of miles away in Texas. She loved to draw and create characters. When she was a teenager, God gave her the idea of a Christian comic book series, and she started to imagine brave, beautiful, and heroic characters in an ethereal land. Her use of metaphor would impress C.S. Lewis while remaining hidden enough to please J.R.R. Tolkien. Without knowing my mom, Leigha, too, would choose an education aligned with her childhood play. She went to art school and majored in Illustration, choosing to focus her coursework on comic book creation.

However, like many of us, her student loans cloaked her graduation with the dread of adulting. She went about her life, comic book notes and sketches collecting dust in a box, and characters' stories collecting dust in her mind.

When we met Leigha, she started telling us about her social media group and the generic positive messaging she was putting into the world. We were trying to dig into why this social media campaign mattered to her. One of us asked, "What happened in your life that led you to this project?" Suddenly, the tone shifted.

"Actually, that's not really what I care about," she said as if shaking cobwebs from her head. "I really want to write and illustrate my own comics. I have one I started when I was fifteen, and I want to finish it."

That was the coolest thing we had ever heard someone say. It wasn't what she said (although writing and illustrating a comic is super cool); it was the way her entire face and body changed when she said it. It was a moment we could see the shift from a "good idea" to a *God Idea*. The Lord was clearly lighting her up from the inside out.

Over the next several months, our conversations with her clarified the problem she saw in the world and who that problem was affecting. She lamented over how many Christians live unaware of the realities of spiritual warfare. This oblivion results in Christians failing to equip the spiritual armor God has given them, and they are left vulnerable to the enemy's attacks.

Leigha's new clarity rekindled her passion to write and illustrate, but she quickly recognized how much time and energy her job consumed. It slowed her down, lessening the compulsion with which she felt God was urging her to make the comic book. She was already dedicating one day per week to working on her own art, but the pressure and demands of her job left her too drained to make much progress.

Something had to give in her work life, and Leigha had a decision to make. She could look for another well-paying job in project management and keep doing art on the side, or she could make the scarier move to develop her own freelance business and do art at her eager pace full time.

She had done freelance work before and never wanted to go back to it, but we've seen *God Ideas* show up like this before. When you don't want to do something you know is good but scary, but you can't stop thinking about it, that might be a *God Idea*. She eventually submitted to God's pull to leave that company altogether and dedicated herself to freelance art and design.

It didn't make sense. Even if the job she had was going to let her go, she could have found another job to ensure bills got paid. Choosing freelance art and design where nothing is certain? Sounds crazy. Writing and illustrating a comic book series? Sounds like that takes a long time. She decided to pour more time into this project, which had no promise of generating an income anytime soon. To many, that seemed like a rash, shortsighted decision. Even Leigha herself questioned it.

The gap

What's stopping you from taking a step toward that scary *God Idea*? If you're like many people, your list of reasons might look like this:

I don't have the money to get started.

I don't know how I'll make the money I need.

The timing isn't right (I have young kids, I just moved, it's a stressful season)

I don't have the skills I think they need (I'm not a good writer, I don't know how to make a website, I don't like speaking in public)

I don't have the equipment I need.

What I have isn't good enough.

I don't know enough people.

I need to quit my job, but I can't.

I don't know how it will all pan out in the end.

I simply don't know what to do next.

It only takes one of those to put off taking action. But did you notice what all of those reasons have in common? They all have something to do with *lack*. A lack of clarity, resources (including time), or experience. We perceive a gap between what we have, and what we think we should have. Like jumping across a large crack in the ground, the wider the gap, the more we hesitate.

At one point, I had written here, "God doesn't see a gap," but I don't think that's true. I'm reminded of Matthew 19, and a conversation Jesus had with a rich young man about how to enter the kingdom of heaven. After the man had expressed his credentials in living a moral life, Jesus noticed a gap. This man had every resource and connection and reputation he needed to accomplish his goals, but he lacked one thing to truly be able to follow Jesus. Jesus encouraged him to exchange his material wealth for treasure in heaven by selling everything he had, and then follow him. When the man saw the gap Jesus identified, he shook his head sadly and walked away. He couldn't take the leap.

Jesus' disciples were shocked that even someone with all those resources and moral backing couldn't enter the kingdom. They asked him, "If even this guy can't be saved, how can anyone?"

And here's how I know Jesus sees the gap between where you are and where you want to be: "Jesus looked at them intently and said, 'Humanly speaking, it is impossible. But with God everything is possible'" (Matthew 19:26).

Not only does God see the gap you see, He jumps into it. God delights in standing in impossible gaps to make a way.

Of course, the way forward is not always obvious to us. You still may see a gap. To share God's heart to repair what's broken, don't focus on the gap. Focus on God's ability to do the impossible, and take the next *imperfect step*.

NOT ONLY DOES GOD SEE THE GAP YOU SEE, HE JUMPS INTO IT.

The next imperfect step

I chose those words intentionally. The next imperfect step.

Next ... because you may not know the next five steps in a row. But you can know the next one.

Imperfect ... because perfection is a fantasy designed to keep you feeling stuck, guilty, and discontent. And God is big enough to work with your half-baked, less-than-ideal contributions.

Step ... because faith is something you *walk*, not just something you *feel*.

Your next imperfect step might require starting something you have no experience in, moving, quitting your job like Leigha, or all of the above like Nehemiah.

Frankly, Leigha isn't the only person we personally know who left the predictability and assurance of a job in response to a *yes* to God.

Darla prayed for a job offer that could serve as a safety net so she could finally leave her toxic work environment. God helped her realize *He* was her safety net, and she needed to jump to Him first. She quit her job, and within weeks, He provided a job better than she imagined.

Chellie knew she needed to quit her job, but was worried about the conflict that would arise with her boss. We prayed with her, she scheduled the meeting, and now she's living the freedom of her faith-filled step (By the way, the conflict she was afraid of didn't even happen)!

Hope worked for a small church. She did everything from answering the phone, to designing graphics, to running social media, to walking the pastor's dog. Sadly, there was no joy or fulfillment in her work, and it began to affect her attitude toward church in general. After hearing us talk about some of these kinds of faith leaps, she reached out to Kelsey and found the courage to trust that God would provide for her and heal her worn-out spirit. She moved to another state, and began working in a "dream job," helping churches grow in healthy and sustainable ways.

Chris had a thriving construction business but knew God was leading him to develop overseas missions and local Kingdom-building work with his wife, Anna. She had turned a pottery-making hobby into a business, and recognizing the potential of Anna's talent and their shared vision for a purpose-driven enterprise, Chris made the big decision to join forces with his wife and pursue ceramics full-time. It didn't make sense financially, but Chris knew he needed to commit fully to God's work. So, he closed down his business and all his other entrepreneurial endeavors to focus solely on the opportunities God presented to them.

Little did they know, that faith leap was only a stepping stone in God's eyes, as he soon called them to a larger, scarier move: close their ceramics business, sell their home in the rural foothills of New Hampshire, and live with their four kids in Tanzania for 10-11 months per year. They are now the directors of Sozo Tanzania, where they reunite families torn apart by poverty, and restore hope to the villagers of Misungwe through Jesus Christ. The inexplicable ways God has provided for their family of six would leave you speechless— you wouldn't even believe half the stories if we wrote them here. And none of them would have come to pass without that first imperfect step.

To be clear, we're not saying you have to quit your job to do Kingdom work. It very well may be that your corporate or secular job is exactly where God will use you to do His work in the world. However, we're also not saying that quitting your job won't be your *next imperfect step* at some point on this journey. We're simply encouraging you to trust that that step will find solid ground when prompted by the Holy Spirit, no matter how scary it may seem. When our friends did take that faith-filled leap, they discovered first-hand that God was both nudging them from behind, and catching them on the other side.

Imperfect but together

We'll often ask our daughter to help us unload the dishwasher. She stacks her cups and bowl and tucks them away in the lower cabinet. She will reach up on her tiptoes and put away glasses, sometimes in the wrong spot, sometimes breaking one in the process. She sorts the silverware more meticulously than is necessary. She's grown more adept as she's gotten older, but we don't *need* her help. In her younger years, she even slowed us down. Inviting her to do the chore with us wasn't for our own efficiency. We invited her for her sake, so she can learn and develop, and—more importantly—so we can spend time together.

You know what? God could have moved all the stones into place and magically assembled the wall of Jerusalem Himself, bigger and better than before. Everyone would have oohed and aahed. But God, like a good and patient father, invited Nehemiah to play a key role in the building of His temple. It wasn't simply about completing the project. It was about growing closer to Him and developing a heart like His through the work.

You may put things in the wrong spot. You may break things in the process. You may spend more time on something than is necessary. That's okay. At least you'll be doing something, and you won't be doing it alone. "I am with you," the Lord said to His people in the beginning of this Jerusalem project, in Haggai 1:13. God promises to be with you as you take your scary, imperfect steps.

See Appendix D to help fight against the urge to take the "perfect" step, and instead identify areas where you can take an imperfect one.

Chapter Five

The Rallying Vision

N ehemiah must have spent the majority of the trip envisioning the state of the city. He replayed the report over and over in his head, "The wall of Jerusalem has been torn down, and the gates have been destroyed by fire." Maybe it was better than he thought. Maybe it was worse. What if there wasn't a city to return to at all?

When Nehemiah arrived in Jerusalem, he wanted to see for himself the extent of the damage. How bad had it gotten? What project had he gotten himself into?

> I slipped out during the night, taking only a few others
> with me. I had not told anyone about the plans God
> had put in my heart for Jerusalem. We took no pack
> animals with us except the donkey I was riding. After
> dark I went out through the Valley Gate, past the
> Jackal's Well, and over to the Dung Gate to inspect
> the broken walls and burned gates. Then I went to the

Fountain Gate and to the King's Pool, but my donkey
couldn't get through the rubble (Neh. 2:11-14).

Your heart has broken for the people. You have identified the problem. You've prayerfully taken an imperfect step in the right direction, even if you don't have all the information. Now it's time to seek more information, and face the undesirable reality of the problem. What exactly are you dealing with?

Sitting across from Chelsea as she laughs, her blue eyes sparkling and her blonde hair cascading down her shoulders, you wouldn't know the weight those shoulders carried on a daily basis. There are precious few people in this world who hear about a problem, fall in love with the people, and stop at nothing to help them, quite like Chelsea Gannon.

Most of us spend crazy numbers of hours late at night mindlessly browsing our phones. I (Kelsey), for example, like watching bunny videos on social media. It's rare that "doom scrolling" brings about lasting, positive change. But for Chelsea, one such evening changed her life.

One night, while browsing her phone, she came across the statistic released by the FBI that 60% of the victims rescued from sex trafficking were at one time in the foster care system. That one statistic embedded itself so deeply in her heart, she would never be the same. She could no longer keep going with life as usual, building her home, raising her kids, attending church and working a job like all she had to live for was the next Disney vacation. There's something broken in the foster care system that loses so many girls to waiting predators, and she grew determined to fix it.

After learning that 90% of girls who age out of foster care will end up homeless, pregnant, or incarcerated by the time they turn 21, Chelsea set to work to change those statistics. She didn't know all the ins and outs of the system, she didn't have a social work degree or experience working with trauma victims; she didn't have funds and programs in place. She just knew she couldn't do nothing.

She started a nonprofit organization called RISE Women and Children. In 2022, bright-eyed and hope-filled, RISE opened a home for women and children and launched an eighteen-month pilot program. It was the biggest, most beautiful move of imperfect action we've ever witnessed. They didn't realize how unprepared they were, but it didn't stop them.

They opened their doors and provided housing to twelve women and children. From there, they helped those women find and keep jobs, move into their own apartments, and restore hope for their futures. They also encountered unimaginable difficulty as they lived side-by-side with women and children who had seen the worst of this world.

In the thick of a New England blizzard, Chelsea's team drove to pick up the first resident of the new RISE home. It was one thing to know the statistic that sparked Chelsea's vision—that 90% of girls who age out of foster care end up homeless, pregnant, or incarcerated by age twenty-one—but this was not a number. In front of them was Chloe. All her belongings fit in one bag. She was homeless, pregnant, and sleeping on the couch of a man she barely knew. Chloe was 18, only barely aged out of foster care.

Chelsea could not have known how hard it would be to walk alongside these women through the trauma they had experienced. Yet, through countless tears, sleepless nights, and broken hearts, Chelsea and her team of dedicated volunteers kept going, compelled by love for these people with a problem too big for Chelsea to fix on her own.

The pilot program showed Chelsea and her team that the need is great; the problem is huge. It was clear they were doing valuable, necessary work in their community. It also demonstrated cracks in their plans, holes in their understanding, and illuminated mistakes they didn't realize they were making. But most importantly, those statistics turned into faces. It wasn't just "90%" anymore. It was Chloe who needed a bed. It was Chloe who they drove to the hospital when it was time for her baby to be born. It was Chloe and her newborn daughter being brought back to the RISE home. For Chelsea, walking with real women in real situations stirred the fire in her that years of study and preparation could not.

As of the writing of this book, Chelsea and her team at RISE are surveying the lessons they learned. The pilot program ended and they're preparing to open a permanent facility. They are establishing relationships with businesses and local organizations. They are having discussions with the department of human services, and local law enforcement and foster care case workers so the next time they open the RISE home, they'll be even more prepared to help the next twelve women and children, and beyond.

As Nehemiah took a tour of the devastation in Jerusalem and Chelsea's team navigated the intricacies of the foster care system, we need to become aware of the extent of the problem we're stepping into. This could look like researching other studies on the topic. You could have conversations with people currently affected by the problem you see and people who are also working to solve it. The problem may be deeply rooted in your heart, or in the hair may require some tough introspection or conversation. You may do a combination of all the above. Whatever your "tour of the problem" looks like, you'll be asking yourself some key questions:

What exists that I could build on?

What organizations or solutions already exist to address the problem? Please understand, this is not to discourage you from moving forward. Your unique perspective is necessary and valuable, and God has positioned you to offer it (Satan will try to convince you your work isn't necessary). Rather, when you identify what is already being done, you have a better understanding of where there are gaps, what you could improve, what would be redundant, and what has been working well.

How does this affect people living in and around it?

The problem wasn't simply the fact that the wall was broken. The problem was what the wall (and the lack thereof) represented. The wall represented safety from wild animals and enemy troops. It offered a high vantage point to be able to spot danger ahead of time. Without a wall, the enemy could slip in without much resistance. The city would be no different than the harsh world outside the walls.

The problem you see is what is keeping people from living a better, safer life. What is the way life *should* be for the people, and how has the problem prevented them from living it?

How does this problem affect me, personally?

One of the ways God creates beauty from the ashes of pain is by walking with you through your pain so you can experience the comfort He offers. Then, you can reach out to share that comfort with others (see 2 Corinthians 1:4).

You might ask, if He's a loving God, why doesn't He comfort each person directly? I'll respond with another question: Is it any less loving if His comfort comes from through one of His willing image-bearers? You see, His comfort is available to everyone, but not everyone leans into Him through their pain. They *may*, however, lean in and listen to *you*. Furthermore, when you share Jesus' comfort with someone, it's a double blessing: they receive comfort from the Lord, and your faith is built by remembering what God led you through. Isn't it just like God to multiply something good out of something painful?

But to be ready to experience this blessing of shared comfort, you need to take inventory of how the problem has affected—and may continue to affect—you.

Don't forget: It's not primarily about the city. It's about the people. As Nehemiah toured Jerusalem, he discovered broken walls, impassable piles of rubble, and charred, burned gates. These conditions reflect the state of many people's hearts who are living with the oppressive reality of the problem.

What is broken?

This question represents the things in someone's life that used to be whole and healthy, but either through a sudden and traumatic event or through years of neglect, became broken. Relationships, self-confidence, trust, support systems, joy. What in a person's heart and life is broken because of the problem?

And don't believe the fatalistic lie that so often accompanies the word *broken*. Broken may be an observation, but it's not a verdict.

What is blocked?

Access has been cut off to what they need or where they want to go. They are facing obstacles that feel insurmountable. The need and the desire to move forward are still there, but until someone clears the obstacle blocking the way, the person is stuck. What systems or mindsets are blocking people from where they want to be?

What is burned?

This question represents the unfortunate reality that sometimes the problem causes permanent damage. Broken things can be repaired, blocked things can be cleared, but burned things remain burned. God is more than able to replace and heal emotional burn wounds—and He may choose to do so—but often, He allows burns and scars to remain a part of this fallen world in which we live. We have to handle those differently than we'd handle broken or blocked things. What are the burns that remain because of the problem?

Some people will be tempted to skip surveying the damage, eager to move quickly to solve the problem they see. Others will be inclined to get stuck in it, overwhelmed by the magnitude of the problem. Avoid either extreme.

Healthily surveying the damage is crucial for two reasons: (1) this time connects the problem to actual people, so you can better understand how to serve them in meaningful ways, and (2) this perspective makes us feel smaller in light of the big problem. That's not a bad thing! Don't let it discourage or overwhelm you. You need to feel small so you can see God as the true solution, and He can be glorified throughout your work.

YOU NEED TO FEEL SMALL SO YOU CAN SEE GOD AS THE TRUE SOLUTION.

Did you notice how Nehemiah hadn't yet said anything to the public? "I had not told anyone about the plans God had put in my heart for Jerusalem" (Neh. 2:12). Later, he re-emphasizes, "The city officials did not know I had been out there or what I was doing, for I had not yet said anything to anyone about my plans" (Neh. 2:14).

There will come a time to announce what God has put on your heart. There is great power in opening your mouth about your Kingdom-building work. But because of that fact, Nehemiah chose his moment wisely. He surveyed the damage privately, quietly. He didn't announce himself as a leader or visionary or entrepreneur. He didn't want anyone to get an inaccurate impression of his role until he had an accurate impression of the work ahead. Only then was it time to make an announcement.

Casting a vision

"But now I said to them, 'You know very well what trouble we are in. Jerusalem lies in ruins, and its gates have been destroyed by fire. Let us rebuild the wall of Jerusalem and end this disgrace!'" (Neh. 2:17)

You are likely to find a vision statement on the wall in your church's lobby, posted in the break room at your workplace, or on the homepage of your favorite nonprofit's website. A vision statement looks ahead at a brighter future and rallies people around to support the pursuit of it. It's like pointing to the mountaintop and saying, "There! That's where we're headed!"

If you don't fancy yourself as an entrepreneur, you don't intend to launch an organization or business, and especially if you aren't leading any other people, it's easy to brush past the corporate-sounding idea of articulating a vision statement. However, crafting a vision statement is a key piece of your Kingdom-building work because, without it, you will find yourself drifting off-course, pursuing opportunities, and opening doors that seem promising and may even be good, but don't draw you closer to the goal.

Your vision statement is also what will stir others to want to support you and your work, regardless of whether or not you lead a team, so you don't have to labor alone.

Chelsea's vision for RISE is this: "Rise will embrace all women, provide education and resources to overcome the hardships they have faced, and empower them to live a life of self-sufficiency." It helps steer the ship and make decisions when opportunities arise. It tells those organizations and businesses that would partner with RISE that they've found the right place. And it reminds every board member and volunteer what they're working for.

What about you? Do you know where you're headed? Even better, can you articulate it clearly? A muddy, wordy vision is hardly a vision at all.

Nehemiah's vision statement provides a helpful template for you to craft your own. In Appendix E, we've provided some steps to do exactly that. The process of arriving at a vision statement is even more important than the vision statement itself, so don't rush it.

Chapter Six

The Inevitable Attacks

Last chapter, we encouraged you to create a vision statement. Vision brings clarity. Clarity opens the door to action. Action builds momentum. Momentum gets results. That's exciting! For you and for the people who catch your vision, the vision statement is like a gunshot to signal the start of the race. You've prepared for the race, you see the finish line, and you're determined to reach it. Yes!

But not everyone is excited about your vision. Not everyone wants you to have clarity and take action and build momentum and ultimately complete the work. Some people want things to stay the way they are. Some people see your breakthrough as a problem.

Nehemiah didn't make much progress before he encountered resistance. Don't expect your journey to be any different. God has an enemy who is literally hell-bent on a mission to hamper, slow, distract, kill, and destroy every good work and willing worker. Let's study what Nehemiah was up against, and how he responded. You will need to repeat this regularly. It means the difference between running the race and running out of steam.

> Sanballat was very angry when he learned that we were rebuilding the wall. He flew into a rage and mocked the Jews, saying in front of his friends and the Samarian army officers, "What does this bunch of poor, feeble Jews think they're doing? Do they think they can build the wall in a single day by just offering a few sacrifices? Do they actually think they can make something of stones from the rubbish heap—and charred ones at that?" Tobiah the Ammonite, who was standing beside him, remarked, "That stone wall would collapse if even a fox walked along the top of it!" (Neh. 4:1-3)

Let's be clear before we unpack this discouraging (and frankly, mean) mess of resistance. You have an enemy watching you work on building God's Kingdom. Jesus faced opposition the entire time He was on earth. In fact, when talking about the opposition He faced, Jesus said, "The thief's purpose is to steal and kill and destroy. My purpose is to give them a rich and satisfying life" (John 10:10).

NOT EVERYONE IS EXCITED ABOUT YOUR VISION.

The thief to which Jesus was referring is His adversary (and ours), Satan. Jesus' purpose is to give people a rich and satisfying life. Your work in Jesus' name, at its core, is showing people such a life is possible through Him. You are continuing Jesus' work two thousand years later. So don't be surprised when Satan concocts various ways to steal your joy, kill your work before it's complete, and destroy the lives and reputations of everyone involved.

The northeastern United States doesn't typically need to brace for hurricanes, but Hurricane Lee was forcing New Englanders to pay attention in September of 2023. It had been slinking east and away from the coastline, downgrading to a tropical storm, but the wind and rain would be felt for miles inland. We partnered with our friend Tracy to spend a week praying for the storm to dissipate, and for God to open up a sunny Saturday in the city where she lives. In a small park in the middle of the city, vendors from across the region and musicians from across the country were expecting to enjoy the last days of summer weather with a faith-based music festival for the community: Revival Day of Hope.

The 2023 event would be the third annual. The festival first sprung from Tracy's heart when travel restrictions in 2020 derailed her regular overseas mission work. It didn't take long before she became aware of the fact that this event was bigger than her. Her enemy wanted her to know it, too.

"That's a lot to take on for one person," she heard from voices both inside and outside her head. "Who are you to build something like this?"

"You're not that organized, this is bound to fail."

Insecurities from inside and out chipped away at her confidence, forcing Tracy to fight harder than ever to keep her music festival going.

On top of the growing weight of Revival Day of Hope, Tracy also made the difficult decision weeks prior to take a sabbatical from her job as a medical department administrator. The job was toxic, and she needed to release it for a time.

That decision allowed more time at home with her mother, for whom she was the full-time caregiver. Tracy knew her mom was in the end-of-life stages, but an unexpected visit to the hospital the Tuesday before Revival Day of Hope solemnly indicated how close she was. Five days before the event—the God-given, Jesus-glorifying event built to usher hope and praise into a city that so desperately needed it—Tracy felt like she was fighting a losing battle on multiple fronts.

The rest of that week was a sleepless one. Tracy wrestled in her heart and mind. She knew she needed to lead Revival Day of Hope through a literal storm. On the other side of the coin, managing Saturday's event meant leaving her mother's bedside, and potentially missing her mother's passing. Tracy resolved with obedient heartache that she would be faithful to steward the scheduled day of the festival and entrust the uncertain day of her mother's passing to God. So, with a heavy heart, she resumed preparations for Revival Day of Hope.

The night before the event, the mobile stage was partially erected in case the storm abated. Such progress filled the onlooking community with excitement. "Looks like this is happening after all," they cheered!

Hurricane Lee did not peel away from New England, however. Its unwelcome hug pummeled the coastal area with 100-mile-an-hour winds and sheets of rain. While we know God heard our prayers for Tracy, He also chose not to follow our script.

When Tracy arrived on site early Saturday, the production crew told her they couldn't finish setting up the stage in these weather conditions. The winds were well above the limits of safety for their crew and the attendees.

Tracy assessed the situation. Artists were already flying in from around the country. Several vendors who hadn't yet canceled had begun driving. And this storm was only escalating, threatening the safety of her team, the crew, the performers, the vendors, and the faithful people who would attend rain or shine. At the risk of upsetting vendors, artists, volunteers, and financial donors, Tracy came to one painful conclusion: she had to cancel Revival Day of Hope.

A small circle of friends on site prayed with Tracy in the rain and helped clean up a few things before they blew away. Then she drove home, changed her clothes, and continued to the hospital. Then, at 5:05 that evening, when the festival would have been underway, we received her text: "My mom just very peacefully passed."

Many might be inclined here, as were those around Tracy at the time, to say, "God worked everything out! The event got canceled so she could be with her mom when her mom passed. How great!" But simplifying the situation felt incomplete and wasn't particularly comforting. The God that "worked everything out" is the same God who could have stopped the hurricane *and* kept Tracy's mom alive for another day. Wouldn't it have been best to allow Tracy to serve the community *and* be with her mom?

We don't know the answer to that. We have to sit with the hard stuff. We have to accept that God's definition of "best" is different from ours.

In a matter of days surrounding this event, everything Tracy had been responsible for was gone: her job, her passion project, her mother. We're not sugarcoating this for you. When you choose to step out and actually do the thing God has put in front of you to do, there will be opposition. Choosing to live by God's script and His design for your life, putting aside your own ambition and desires, and seeking first the Kingdom and His righteousness is not a quick fix to your problems. In truth, it will introduce a host of new challenges. Your *yes* to work with God to heal what's broken will unleash an army of *no*s against you: physical, spiritual, natural, and emotional. And they don't play fair.

Jesus walking on water is one of those miracles that even non-Christians know. "She thinks she walks on water" has become a euphemism for someone thinking they're perfect. The story is recorded in Matthew chapter 14, and in case you haven't read it in a while, here's the scene: Jesus and His disciples had just spent the day with crowds. They had tried to get away to some peace and quiet, but when the crowds followed, Jesus and His friends continued to serve and teach them. That night, dinner time came around and with no more than two loaves of bread and five fish, Jesus performed another famous miracle—feeding over 5,000 men and their families.

After this miracle, Jesus needed some serious recoup time. Fellow introverts know the feeling, "I love you dearly; please go away." He sent His disciples in a boat to cross the sea, out of reach of the crowds. And He went up to a mountain to get the time alone to pray and restore His soul.

In the middle of the night, the disciples fought Hurricane Lee-like wind and waves from the diminishing safety of their little fishing boat. Over the waves, highlighted by frequent flashes of lightning, they saw what looked like a man walking toward them on the water! They freaked out, thinking it was a ghost, because fear leads to more fear. Then one of the most jaw-dropping moments in all of Scripture happens:

But Jesus spoke to them at once. "Don't be afraid," he said. "Take courage. I am here!"

Then Peter called to him, "Lord, if it's really you, tell me to come to you, walking on the water."

"Yes, come," Jesus said.

So Peter went over the side of the boat and walked on the water toward Jesus (Matthew 14:27-29).

Peter *walked on water*. He did it! Sure, everyone talks about how the next sentence tells us he sank when he took his eyes off Jesus. His focus was on the waves, and he needed Jesus to pull him up and get him into the boat. But first—Peter *walked on water!*

Isn't it interesting that this miracle didn't happen on a calm, warm night when the disciples were relaxed? Can you picture that? Peter is repairing some nets, and Matthew is updating his journal. Thaddeus and Nathaniel drift asleep. John and James are bickering over who gets to steer. Andrew is playing the ukelele.

Then Philip leans over to splash some water on his face and sees a reflection. It's Jesus! And he's standing on the water!

"Hey guys! Having fun?" Jesus calls out.

"Whoa! How are you doing that?"

"Come on in, the water's fine!" invites their teacher.

Peter is first. He puts one leg over the edge of the boat, shifts his weight onto the glassy-smooth lake, and practically giggles in delight. "Guys! This is amazing! You gotta try it!"

Then his brother, Andrew, grabs Peter with one hand and his ukelele with the other as he steps out of the boat. One by one, they all dance like children in the splash park as the fish sing "sha-la-la-la-la" in the moonlight.

Of course, that's not how things went down. Jesus came to them when they were already surrounded by problems. The wind was gusty. The boat was tossed by the waves. They were already fighting for their lives.

Peter had an idea to do something that made no sense given their circumstances. "Tell me to come to you, walking on the water." And Jesus agreed! Peter had taken to heart when Jesus told them to have courage because "I am here." So much courage, that he asked to do something crazy. And Jesus welcomed it. Jesus was in control of all the mess around them, but He didn't stop it all before calling Peter out of the boat and enabling him to do something no one had ever done before and no one has done since.

Jesus is in your mess, too. He's not asking you to step into something new amidst calm seas and perfectly manicured lives. He's asking you to do things that don't make sense in the middle of all the other stuff of life that's already hard. All the stuff you're currently dealing with in your family, your work, your finances, your relationships, your church, your inner mind—all that isn't going anywhere. Yet, Jesus is *still* inviting you into something with *Him* that doesn't make sense. There will be trouble, conflict, and resistance. *Do not expect these things to calm down before you step out of the boat. Step anyway.*

Satan is mean.

Let that be the blunt understatement it is. He doesn't play fair. He picks moments and uses people he knows will hurt the most. He attacks from different angles. He distracts you on one side, and while you are dealing with that, he infiltrates another area of your life, if you're not careful.

Remember what Nehemiah's enemies said? "What does this bunch of poor, feeble Jews think they're doing? Do they think they can build the wall in a single day by just offering a few sacrifices? Do they actually think they can make something of stones from the rubbish heap—and charred ones at that?" Tobiah the Ammonite, who was standing beside him, remarked, "That stone wall would collapse if even a fox walked along the top of it!" (Neh. 4:1-3)

Satan is mean

Look at the types of attacks Satan launched through various people watching Nehemiah.

> **He demeaned the Jews' value** ("poor")
>
> **He belittled their strength.** ("feeble")
>
> **He questioned their clarity.** ("What do they think they're doing?")
>
> **He misrepresented their goal.** ("build the wall in a single day?")
>
> **He challenged their faith.** ("...just by offering a few sacrifices?")
>
> **He over-simplified their project.** ("something of stones")
>
> **He over-emphasized their problem.** ("rubbish heap—and charred ones at that!")
>
> **He disparaged their quality.** ("it would collapse")

Have you experienced doubt and discouragements like those? Likely, you've thought or heard similar ideas ever since God put His work on your heart. God isn't the only one trying to tell you something. Your enemy wants his ideas to get some airtime in your mind. Before you lay even one proverbial brick in your "wall" of Kingdom work, you need to recognize the primary battle is not in front of you. It's in your mind.

Who's talking?

After Tracy canceled her event and she lost her mom, the accusations came pouring in.

"You only canceled the event because your mom was sick. It was a bad business decision."

"You're only doing this event for your own glory; if you really had faith in Jesus, He would have stopped the rain *and* healed your mom!"

"You didn't trust God enough!"

"Canceling the event was selfish!"

"You waited too long to cancel."

"You canceled too soon."

"You handled it all wrong."

Whenever you submit to God's plans and will for your life, you will hear a lot of opinions from a lot of people. Voices will flood your ears.

When Jesus was referring to Satan's goal to "steal, kill, and destroy" like we mentioned earlier, He was not making friends. He was accusing the religious leaders of being false teachers—voices that would lead His people astray. Jesus called Himself the good shepherd, and His people (that includes you and me) are His sheep. That's not exactly a compliment.

Sheep wander off, they get distracted, they're often stubborn, and they fall into the same traps again and again. They might feel independent, but they are truly made to be led by a shepherd. Does any of that sound painfully familiar? However, there is one thing sheep do particularly well. They recognize the voice of their shepherd, and they ignore the voices of anyone else trying to call them. They know who they can trust, they know who's there to protect them, and they follow that voice.

Jesus continues the sheep/shepherd metaphor, "He goes on ahead of them, and his sheep follow him because they know his voice. But they will never follow a stranger; in fact, they will run away from him because they do not recognize a stranger's voice" (John 10:4-5).

If you are going to follow Jesus, you need to learn how to discern between His voice and strangers' voices. The two most common types of interfering voices are *discouragement* and *doubt*.

Opposition 1: Discouragement

"Discourage" literally means "to remove the courage from". Whether it comes from a close friend or relative who doesn't catch your vision, or from a thoughtless stranger on the internet, words can suck the excitement out of your next steps. Words have the power to deplete whatever courage you may have. Regardless of who speaks (or types) the discouraging words, discouragement is Satan's attempt to prevent you from having the courage to obey God.

Even one of Jesus' best friends was Satan's mouthpiece in a moment of discouragement. As Jesus was sharing His mission with His disciples—how He would have to suffer and die and be raised to life again—Peter responded with what he thought was encouragement, "No! Not you! This won't happen to you!"

Jesus' response must have felt like a jolt of electricity, "Get away from me, Satan! You are a dangerous trap to me. You are seeing things merely from a human point of view, not from God's" (Matthew 16:23).

Peter may have thought he was encouraging or protecting his friend, but in truth, he was discouraging Jesus from moving forward with His mission. Satan is the ultimate source of discouragement, and it is a dangerous trap for the Kingdom-minded Christ-follower.

Opposition 2: Doubt

While discouragement is like litter that others toss into our mental space, doubt is the clutter that accumulates when we don't take the time to throw it away. Discouragement is a seed; doubt is discouragement that has grown roots. We doubt when we start to entertain and believe the discouragements that come our way.

Discouragements from Sanballat transformed into doubt in the minds of the Jewish workers. "The people of Judah began to complain, 'The workers are getting tired, and there is so much rubble to be moved. We will never be able to build the wall by ourselves'" (Neh. 4:10).

Do you recognize how eerily similar the workers' own thoughts were to Sanballat's accusations? His discouragements were allowed to grow roots. His words found accepting hearts, discouragement mutated into doubt.

"You can't do that. How are you going to provide for your family?" is a discouragement from a well-meaning aunt.

"I can't do this; it won't make any money" is a home-grown, locally-sourced, farm-to-table doubt. Doubts are harder to shake because, at some level, you actually believe them to be true.

James warns that a believer who doubts is like a wave tossed around like the wind (James 1:6). That is, if discouragement is able to knock you off course and weigh on your mind as a doubt, the next discouragement that comes along is likely to do the same. Truth steadies the ship and keeps it on course.

Tuning in

Discouragement is the external voices that don't align with your mission. Doubt is your internal voice echoing those discouragements after the fact. It doesn't take much to create a cacophony in your mind! Once you've become aware of the voices around you, your response should be that of a master sound engineer: turn the volume down on the channels that aren't contributing to the main focus, and turn the volume up on the channels that need our attention.

Tracy's experience was painful. However, through it all, she experienced a closeness with her Savior like never before. She has tuned her heart to hear His voice and He continues to say, "abide." In the rubble of all she lost she has found strength and peace as she continues to abide in her Heavenly Father.

Nehemiah's first response in light of the enemy's voice was to get on God's channel.

"Then I prayed, 'Hear us, our God, for we are being mocked. May their scoffing fall back on their own heads, and may they themselves become captives in a foreign land! Do not ignore their guilt. Do not blot out their sins, for they have provoked you to anger here in front of the builders'" (Neh. 4:4).

Remember, in John 10, Jesus explained that His sheep know His voice, and they run away from anyone who is not their shepherd. Please understand—as we are continually trying to understand better—your success as a Kingdom-building Christ-follower is directly related to your ability to tune into God's voice. You are not going about this work alone. God is working with you, and God is working on you.

"For we are both God's workers," Paul says in 1 Corinthians 3:9, "and you are God's field. You are God's building."

How do you distinguish between God's voice and all the other voices floating around? It's intensely personal and requires you to spend time with Jesus to know how He speaks with you as His worker (which is the point, ultimately). But here are some things that will always be true.

God's voice ...

- is the Bible. All Scripture is God-breathed and useful for teaching, correcting, rebuking, and training (2 Timothy 3:16).

- accompanies your study of the Bible. The Holy Spirit teaches you everything you need to know (1 John 2:27).

- never contradicts the Bible. God doesn't lie or change His mind about what he's promised (Numbers 23:19).

- doesn't sound like your voice. His ways, thoughts, and plans are higher than yours (Isaiah 55:8).

In summary, spend time reading the Bible. Ask God to teach you what you need to know. Filter out the voices that don't line up with what you read. Be wary when an idea sounds too comfortable as if it doesn't take much to believe and act on it. God's ways are higher than yours.

Be warned! *Big yesses acted on in faith will be accompanied by loud voices trying to discourage you from taking another one.*

In these cases, celebrate! Take encouragement from James.

"Dear brothers and sisters, when troubles of any kind come your way, consider it an opportunity for great joy. For you know that when your faith is tested, your endurance has a chance to grow. So let it grow, for when your endurance is fully developed, you will be perfect and complete, needing nothing" (James 1:2-4).

Every victory over discouragement and doubt builds endurance for the next attack.

Oh, and there will be more attacks ...

See Appendix F to form a battle plan from Scripture (specifically Philippians 4:8) to combat Satan's attacks on your mind. Seriously, this is good stuff.

Chapter Seven

The Escalating Tactics

"**M**eanwhile, our enemies were saying, 'Before they know what's happening, we will swoop down on them and kill them and end their work'" (Neh. 4:11).

Whoa, now! That escalated quickly! Sanballat wasn't content with his jeers and boos from the sidelines. The wall was still being built! The discouragements weren't penetrating the workers' hearts as deeply as he had hoped, so he had to change tactics. *If the doubts and discouragements don't stop you from working, don't expect your enemy to back off. In fact, expect it to get worse.*

We see a progression when it comes to opposition to your Kingdom-building mission. The first two phases were (1) discouragement and (2) doubt. The next two are (3) direct attacks and (4) distractions.

Opposition 3: Direct Attacks

Satan hates you.

You personally. "Why? What did I ever do to him?"

It's not about what you do to him; it's about what God does for you. God loves you. You personally! He gave you free will and the ability to choose to love Him and serve Him. When you do, it's another slap in the face of the narcissistic poser who wants so desperately to be God. So yeah, Satan hates you. He thinks you're weak and pathetic and ugly. But the truth is, the thing God asked you to do is so dangerous to Satan's mission, that he's dead set on taking you and your work down as soon as possible.

And yes, it's personal.

Dear Kingdom-building friends of ours have experienced personal and direct attacks against their marriage, their health, their spouse, their kids, their volunteers and employees, their finances, their homes, and their reputations. It feels like open season on anyone trying to follow Jesus.

If there's anybody throughout history that should have been impervious to discouragements and doubts, it was John the Baptist. After all, prophets foretold his birth and purpose hundreds of years earlier. An angel came to announce his existence and name to his parents. He recognized the Spirit of Jesus while they were both still in their mothers' wombs. John had one mission: to declare that Jesus was the Messiah, the savior of the world. Boom. Crystal clear. End of discussion. John was so bold and confident in His mission, he called His enemies snakes to their faces. They couldn't touch him!

Then the direct attacks began. John made some enemies who threw him in prison. And there he sat. Boldly and defiantly at first, no doubt.

"Hah! I won't be here long. My cousin is the Messiah who has come to free us from your tyrannical reign! Wait 'til He gets here. Then you'll be sorry!"

But the more time passed, the more time John had to sit and think about where things could have gone wrong. Maybe he missed something.

"Was I way off? Did I misunderstand the mission? Did I come on too strong? Did I get caught up in the emotion of it? Is Jesus even who He says He is?"

Apparently, the doubts escalated so much, he sent some messengers to ask Jesus if He really was the Messiah they'd been hoping for. Discouragement, doubt, direct attacks—John was the target of all sorts of opposition. Ultimately, the attacks grew so intense (and so personal), it cost John his life when one of his enemies demanded his literal head to be delivered on a platter.

But Jesus knew such direct and personal attacks were merely desperate attempts to stop the rush of God's Kingdom being built on earth.

"I tell you the truth, of all who have ever lived, none is greater than John the Baptist. Yet even the least person in the Kingdom of Heaven is greater than he is! And from the time John the Baptist began preaching until now, *the Kingdom of Heaven has been forcefully advancing, and violent people are attacking it*" (Matthew 11:11-12, emphasis added).

What if what Jesus said about John is true? What if you are even greater than John? Do you suppose Jesus is bragging about you to His friends? While you're busy wondering if you've wasted your time, or if your work makes a difference, could Jesus be saying, "Since they started, God's Kingdom has been making huge strides! So much so, in fact, that the enemy is desperately trying to attack it!"?

Who is the attack actually against?

In the face of direct and personal attacks that threatened their lives, homes, and families, Nehemiah encouraged his people, "Don't be afraid of the enemy! Remember the Lord, who is great and glorious, and fight for your brothers, your sons, your daughters, your wives, and your homes!" (Neh. 4:14)

Remember the problem Nehemiah recognized and wept for early on? The broken wall meant God would be a dishonored laughing stock among the neighboring nations, and the Jewish families would be helplessly targeted by whoever wanted to walk in and harass them. The attacks weren't actually targeting Nehemiah, no matter how personal they felt. Nehemiah recognized the attacks were in fact against God and the people God loved.

When you feel like you have Satan's full, undivided attention, don't give him your attention in return. He doesn't deserve it. Take Nehemiah's rally to heart. Don't be afraid of the enemy. Remember the Lord, who is great and glorious. Fight for the people who will continue to suffer until this work is complete.

Managing the tension of kingdom-building

Check out how Nehemiah instructed his people to work.

> When our enemies heard that we knew of their plans
> and that God had frustrated them, we all returned to
> our work on the wall. From then on, only half my
> men worked while the other half stood guard with
> spears, shields, bows, and coats of mail. The leaders

stationed themselves behind the people of Judah who were building the wall. The laborers carried on their work with one hand supporting their load and one hand holding a weapon. (Neh. 4:15-17)

Well, that's not particularly efficient.

We're sure the Jews worked significantly faster earlier, when half of them didn't have to stand guard, and when builders could use two hands instead of one. But what other choice did they have? They couldn't proceed fully one way or the other. All work-as-usual would have left them vulnerable to attack. All battle-ready would have meant never completing the wall. Either one would spell disaster. Both mindsets, while functionally opposite, had to remain true at the same time. That is an example of tension.

Biblical Christians are no strangers to tension. We are called to declare truth but also extend grace. We must believe God is one God, but also three persons. We understand God is sovereign, but He gave us free will. The two opposites shouldn't both be true, yet they are! In our Kingdom-building work, we find this tension of needing to commit fully to our work while also needing to stand firm in the armor of God with the sword of the Spirit (God's Word), as Paul describes in the sixth chapter of Ephesians.

We can't cut the tension by choosing one way or the other. We've seen too many Christian leaders and artists pour a lifetime of energy and resources into building their ministry while neglecting to guard against Satan's attacks. The result may be a seemingly successful ministry from the outside but a desolate personal life. On the other hand, we know many Christians who read the Bible and pray and have strong relationships (all good things) but are so scared of failing that they don't take any steps to do the work in front of them.

We can't resort to one extreme or the other. Therefore, we have to manage both sides of the tension. What does that look like? Similar to how Nehemiah's men worked, when facing opposition, we need to work with one hand and carry the sword in the other.

- Start your day by reading the Bible instead of checking your inbox.

- Spend more time than you think you can afford in prayer.

- Take a full day of rest, even though the to-do list is only half done.

- Invest time with other believers even when you're tired.

- Meet mid-day with a mentor who will point you to Jesus.

- Keep your promise to your family to be home for dinner even though an extra hour or two on the project feels like it would make all the difference.

- Say "no" to contracts and opportunities that would pull you away from your family, church, or Kingdom work, no matter how much they pay.

GOD'S PACE IS SLOWER THAN YOUR EXPECTATIONS AND FASTER THAN YOUR FAITH.

Let's come to terms with the fact that doing God's work, God's way, in a world where Satan is temporarily let off his leash is not going to be as efficient as you want it to be. *God's pace is slower than your expectations and faster than your faith.* Progress may come slower than you expect, but managing the tension of Kingdom-building is the only way to emerge with the work—and the worker—intact.

Opposition 4: Distractions

> Sanballat, Tobiah, Geshem the Arab, and the rest of our enemies found out that I had finished rebuilding the wall and that no gaps remained—though we had not yet set up the doors in the gates. So Sanballat and Geshem sent a message asking me to meet them at one of the villages in the plain of Ono. But I realized they were plotting to harm me. (Neh. 6:1-2)

Believe it or not, direct personal attacks are not even the most effective weapon against your progress. Your enemy has a final trick up his sleeve. You're on the home stretch now. If you can't be discouraged, if you're not stuck in doubt, and if you are armored up against attacks, then maybe—just maybe—he can distract you.

Distractions are a finely tuned weapon against Kingdom work, a weapon that Satan has spent millennia honing and updating with the times. C.S. Lewis, in his book *The Screwtape Letters*, speaks from the fictional perspective of a veteran demon mentoring a novice demon in the art of keeping a Christian from being an effective worker in God's Kingdom.

> You no longer need a good book, which he really likes, to keep him from his prayers or his work or his sleep; a column of advertisements in yesterday's paper will

do. You can make him waste his time not only in conversation he enjoys with people whom he likes, but in conversations with those he cares nothing about on subjects that bore him. You can make him do nothing at all for long periods. You can keep him up late at night, not roistering, but staring at a dead fire in a cold room. All the healthy and out-going activities which we want him to avoid can be inhibited and *nothing* given in return, so that at least he may say... "I now see that I spent most of my life in doing *neither* what I ought *nor* what I liked."[2]

It doesn't take much imagination to see the modern-day parallels with Lewis' World-War-2-era observations. The more we give in to distractions, the more we can be kept from praying, working, or sleeping by scrolling through ads for items we didn't know existed. We can be convinced to engage in conversations with strangers on the internet about topics that don't matter to us. Eventually, distractions don't have to be as tempting as a fun party at a friend's house; they can be as dull and mundane as staring at a glowing blue screen in a dark room.

Bad, good, and best

What makes distractions such a potent strategy against our work is that they aren't inherently negative, unlike the other oppositions we face (discouragement, doubt, and direct attacks).

Do you want to know what I (Mike) am most often distracted by? Housework. Doing the dishes, vacuuming the rug, folding the laundry. When given the option between writing for a couple of hours or doing chores, I'll probably grab the vacuum. Hear me out: unlike a lot of mental work, I can usually get a quick win and see instant improvement when I do chores. That, at their core, is what distractions offer—a quick win, a bit of progress in something, a little shot of dopamine.

There's nothing negative or wrong about reading a book, doing dishes, or exercising (now *that's* a distraction I don't understand!). Those are all good things. But that's just it—they are *good* things. They're not always the *best* things. If you want to stand a chance against distractions, you'll need to recognize what is bad, what is good, and what is best. Decide *ahead of time* what is best, and everything else will fall short of it. Even good things won't appear as priorities.

And while it may seem obvious that doing your Kingdom work is best, check in with God throughout the process. His idea of *best* may be different than yours. Allow yourself to re-prioritize based on what God puts in front of you. Maybe "best" looks like spending quality time with your family, giving more time to church for a season, or reaching out to someone God has put on your heart. Take care to not develop tunnel vision, so focused on your idea of what needs to be done, that you block out God along with the distractions.

I'm doing great work!

Whenever I have to stay focused for extended periods of time (usually at my computer, writing or recording), I fasten a little sticky note onto the side of my monitor. It contains Nehemiah's response to the distractions he was experiencing: "I'm doing a great work, and I cannot come down!" (Neh. 6:3, ESV)

When you categorize your to-do list and pop-ups as "Bad, Good, and Best", you can be certain about what your "great work" is, and what it's not. When you're doing a great work, why would you possibly come down from that for something not great? Take Nehemiah's response as your own. You might want to write it down like I did, and keep it in front of you when you need to avoid distractions.

Look—you won't reject 100% of distractions. You will "come down" off your wall multiple times over the course of the work. Maybe even multiple times a day. When you do, Satan attempts the double punch: WHAM—get distracted!—BAM—feel guilty about it! If that happens, repent, pray, and get back on that wall.

Take heart, Kingdom-builder. God is doing *His* great work in you and around you; you may not even see it. You may feel sidelined, sidetracked, or blindsided, but the good news is the work God put on your heart is bigger than you. That's the point. You're not supposed to have it all figured out or be able to crush every goal based on your own effort or understanding. You may not be able to see the finish line. The Kingdom of Heaven is forcefully advancing. *It's your race to run; it's God's war to win.*

Keep getting derailed by distractions? See Appendix G to identify and take steps to eliminate distractions in your life.

Chapter Eight

The Supportive Community

With a trowel in one hand and a sword in the other, Nehemiah and the Jewish people reconstructed the walls around the city. They took the ruins from a disorganized pile of rubble to a knee-high stone fence, to a barrier you had to stand on your toes to look over, to the final full-height wall in all its glory, wrapped around the city like a long-awaited hug. Then, undoubtedly with a huge sigh of relief, Nehemiah wrote in his journal, "On October 2 the wall was finished—just fifty-two days after we had begun. When our enemies and the surrounding nations heard about it, they were frightened and humiliated. They realized this work had been done with the help of our God" (Neh. 6:15-16).

That's why God cares about the completion of the project He led you to do: so all the onlookers can realize that it was done with the help of your God. For your spiritual enemies, this will be frightening and humiliating news. For the onlookers who watched from a distance, this will inspire them to lean in and see God more. And for your community of people, this is cause for celebration as you grow closer to each other and to your God.

What follows in Nehemiah's narrative is a lengthy, and frankly tedious record of the names and numbers of the people who were involved in the project. At least, that's how it may seem to us. God told Nehemiah alone to do this mission, but He didn't tell him to do the mission alone. To Nehemiah, each number represented the names and families of co-laborers who linked arms and overcame immeasurable obstacles in pursuit of their God-given vision for the project. Back in Nehemiah 3, Nehemiah began crediting each household for the sections of walls and gates for which they were responsible.

Nehemiah reeled as he remembered the speed and passion with which his friend Baruch worked. "Next to him was Baruch son of Zabbai, who zealously repaired an additional section from the angle to the door of the house of Eliashib the high priest" (Neh. 3:20).

And Shallum? Good gracious, that man was a powerhouse. "The Fountain Gate was repaired by Shallum, son of Col-hozeh, the leader of the Mizpah district. He rebuilt it, roofed it, set up its doors, and installed its bolts and bars. Then he repaired the wall of the pool of Siloam near the king's garden, and he rebuilt the wall as far as the stairs that descend from the City of David" (Neh. 3:15).

Nehemiah shook his head and chuckled in disbelief as he penned verse 29. "Next Zadok son of Immer also rebuilt the wall across from his own house." Even Old Man Zadok got in on the action.

What faithful co-laborers. What loyal supporters. What a vital, life-giving community. When the wall was finally complete, therefore, Nehemiah was proud to take inventory of all the people involved at any level of the project, and all those who would benefit from this great effort.

Your Kingdom work is not a solo project. You may feel alone now, but God has zealous co-workers, enthusiastic supporters, and a faithful community for you.

Roll call

Did you try to read Nehemiah chapters 3, 7, 10, 11, and 12? There are so many names! It reads like a graduation—name after name after name. Reading them feels about as fun as sitting through a graduation. We're going to shoot straight with you, these chapters in Nehemiah are not easy to read. One translation titles a portion of it, "Nehemiah takes a census." However, we highly dislike that title; it sounds too governmental. When we read these lists of men, women, leaders, priests, Levites, musicians, workers, survivors, fighters, and families, we see all the people God brought around Nehemiah to complete the work. Check out how these names are organized:

Chapter 3 provides the names of all the people who had built the wall and their specific roles in doing so (Shout out to the brave men and women who were charged with building the Dung Gate. Someone had to do it). These are **partners**.

Chapter 7 is a list of the people who would build the communities and culture within the walls. These are **cheerleaders**.

Chapter 10 is a list of the people who signed Jerusalem's renewed covenant with God, and would work to help the future generations remain faithful. These are **mentors**.

Chapter 11 is a list of the leaders of the people who resettled to populate Jerusalem. These are **receivers** of the benefits of this project.

Chapter 12 is a history of the people who paved the way for Nehemiah to accomplish all that was being done. These are **predecessors.**

Partners, cheerleaders, mentors, receivers, and predecessors. All that Nehemiah set out to do and all that would continue was the collective effort of a massive community of people. Remember Nehemiah's vision statement?

"Rebuild the wall and end our disgrace."

Your vision statement may feel equally bigger-than-you. He couldn't do it alone, and frankly, even after the wall was rebuilt, it was only the beginning of a new future. The ultimate goal was not to have a physical wall built; the wall was the beginning of re-establishing God's chosen people in the promised land. It was a Kingdom work—not to build the kingdom of Judah, but to build the Kingdom of God within His people. The real project was not one of stone and mortar. The real project was one of bone and marrow, of heart and wholeness. It was bringing people back to Jerusalem, back to the place God wanted them to be to live the way He had always intended for them to live: together. *Building community—being together—is the heart of the project.*

Who is your community?

The work you are doing is not merely about the work. The goal is not to start your thing and finish your thing and then have a thing on a shelf, or on a resume, or available for purchase. The goal of your thing is to draw people back to where God wants them to be, to share His heart. It is to draw people closer into a relationship with Him so they can live their lives the way God knows is best. It's always about the people—and not only your current or future customers or clients. God is offering growth and relationship to the people who come alongside you.

In Appendix H, which corresponds to this chapter, we break down the various types of co-laborers in Nehemiah's circles and use them to identify your existing or potential community. Don't skip this part. The work to anticipate, identify, and celebrate your community will transform the way you pray, prepare, and carry out the work God has given you to do.

BUILDING COMMUNITY IS THE HEART OF THE PROJECT.

You might not have a city to fortify. Maybe contractors and soldiers won't be part of your Kingdom community, but you do have work to do. You have a race to run. Recognize your community. Recognize the people God has placed in your life who are running in the same direction. Look around you. Who's cheering you on? Who's catching your vision? Who's there when things don't go well? Who points you to Jesus to keep going? Lean into those people!

Have you told them yet?

I (Mike) sat with a couple at a church picnic one warm summer afternoon. We were friendly acquaintances, but had not shared much about our lives up to that point. When the conversation turned to asking what Kelsey and I have been up to, I summoned my courage. This was probably the first time I would speak these words out loud, outside the four walls of our home.

"Well, we've been recording a podcast for a couple years where I read the Bible. And now we're working to produce live presentations of entire books of the Bible to perform at churches."

"Wow, sounds incredible! And so important!"

"Yeah, we're looking forward to seeing what God does."

And then came a question I wasn't expecting, "Have you told your church family about this?"

"Um … no, actually. Not yet."

"Oh you definitely should. A lot of people would love to know about this and support you."

These friends were right, of course. Their question highlighted an insecurity of mine that has accompanied every creative project as long as I can remember: I don't like to reveal what I'm working on until it's "ready."

I put *ready* in quotes, of course, because we all know that's a mirage. *Ready* never comes. And I'm not only talking about creative projects or organized work. This mentality shows up even in habits and self-improvement, "I'll work on that to become a better husband. Then when I'm better, Kelsey will be excited to see the new me!" It's laughable to think it's a good plan, but I keep the work-in-progress in the closet until it's complete.

Ridiculous, but relatable, right? I get it. If you keep your project private, you feel protected. If nobody knows about it, nobody can say anything negative about it. If you end up stopping, you haven't disappointed anyone, because no one was anticipating it. And so it stays in your mind or on your shelf, filed under "intentions."

The problem with this strategy is you are depriving yourself of the oxygen God designed for you to work and grow in—community! God tasks His people with the responsibility of creatively sharpening each other: "Let us think of ways to motivate one another to acts of love and good works. And let us not neglect our meeting together, as some people do, but encourage one another, especially now that the day of his return is drawing near" (Hebrews 10:24-25).

Quite simply, if you're waiting until your official launch, release, or reveal before you let yourself or your work become known to fellow believers, you are missing out on God's Plan A for motivation, encouragement, and community.

(Note: watch out for Satan's opposition in the form of, "You're just a shameless self-promoter. Don't talk about your work to your friends." Trust me, if you're worried about coming across as self-promoting, you probably talk about your project *too little*, not too much.)

We took our friends' advice and shared *Outloud Bible Project Podcast* with more friends from church. Our pastor generously invited us to host an Outloud Bible Experience on an upcoming Sunday and invite our church family to support the ministry. Now, when we are in our home church on a Sunday, people will ask us about *Outloud Bible* and where we've been, and share how a podcast episode helped them that week.

My fears about coming across as self-promoting are quelled when I hear how God is working in people's lives through the spoken Word, how they feel more confident to read the Bible on their own, and how putting the Bible into action has healed their relationships with friends and family. And that's just based on what I've seen and heard. I'll never know the full impact. So I had to arrive at this sobering thought: if God invited me to His work, and if God's heart behind it is to reach and restore people ... if I hide from God's community because I don't feel "ready," I'm selfishly making this work about me.

So I'll ask you with the same love in which my friends asked me, "Have you told them yet?"

Dedicate and celebrate

In this chapter, until now, we've assumed you haven't completed your project. The conversation around community has been more future-oriented than descriptive. But sooner or later, or possibly already behind you to some degree, you'll see a victory. It may not be the finished product, but there's something that warrants a celebration.

More than your growth, more than the benefits of completing the project, and more than the tight-knit community, this project is about God. He's infinitely good and creative, all those other areas can flourish over the course of the project, but the main point is, and always will be, God's glory.

That was not lost on Nehemiah and the Jews. In chapter 12, Nehemiah describes a festive parade and uproarious dedication of the new wall. Priests came from across the region. Two choirs marched in different directions. Nehemiah stood atop the wall with his friends. Priests gave speeches. Throughout the day, people sang loudly! "Many sacrifices were offered on that joyous day, for *God had given the people cause for great joy.* The women and children also participated in the celebration, and the joy of the people of Jerusalem could be heard far away" (Neh. 12:43, emphasis added).

If you are a particularly driven individual, you may be tempted to move on to the next pressing project. Or, if it took you every ounce of energy and perseverance to get to this point, you may be tempted to crash and take a three-month-long nap. Either way, do not skip the God-honoring action of dedication and celebration.

Dedicating the project to God in a public and joyful way is an act of humility. It abdicates your right to take credit and gives God the credit for every good thing. It says, "God, you put this on my heart in the first place. You gathered a community of people around it. You carried us through the ups and downs. You are the reason it is complete."

Celebrating the project is to worship God for what He's done. After all, He has given you "cause for great joy." What a shame it would be either to rush onto the next project or crash from this one when God has given you so many reasons to celebrate! Celebration doesn't have to be at the scale of a city-wide parade, of course. It can be a meal, a party, a date night, a letter, or even a conversation. Whatever the scale of the work, celebrate with the community God has placed you in. God has given you cause for great joy!

God may have already placed supportive community members around you in your life. See Appendix H to help identify them.

Chapter Nine

The Messy Reality

If the book of Nehemiah was an epic, inspirational movie, Chapters 10 through 12 served as a sort of credit roll, acknowledging the hundreds of people who were involved in the project. If the story ended there, you might be inspired to charge ahead, believing you have found a proven way to help you "achieve your dreams."

Let's take inventory of Nehemiah's journey of restoring what was broken. You may even recognize yourself somewhere on this path:

> He recognized a **problem** that broke God's heart and his.
>
> He saturated the problem in **prayer** before anything else.
>
> His confidence in God helped him take an **imperfect step**, to move even when he didn't know the big picture.
>
> He surveyed the damage and cast a **vision** to solve it.
>
> He guarded against various types of **opposition** to the project.
>
> He celebrated how his **community** came together to do the Lord's work.

Nice, right? But the book doesn't end there, does it? After neat-and-tidy Chapter 12 comes rough-and-tumble Chapter 13, like a bonus scene after the credits to show us the story continues even after we thought we were done.

Here's the unfortunate truth about Kingdom work: it's messy, rarely linear, and we often have to go back and revisit what we thought had passed. We would be remiss if we ended this book by hyping you up with a seven-chapter process and giving you an exuberant high-five as you set off on your adventure. We have to warn you that your Kingdom work will probably not progress neatly from "identify the problem" to "celebrate your community." Casting a vision may come later than you want it to, the enemy's attacks may come earlier. And imperfect steps aren't only for the starting line; there will be necessary stumbles along the way. But if we had emphasized that early on, it's doubtful you would have gotten this far.

So, since you're still here, and before we conclude, let's check out Nehemiah Chapter 13 for an honest look at the messy, nonlinear steps (and backsteps) you may find yourself taking—not only at the end of the path, but throughout.

Unauthorized access (Nehemiah 13:4-9)

Long ago, God had banned particular groups of foreigners from assembling in the temple. Does that seem intolerant to you? Exclusive?

As a matter of fact, it was. Not because God didn't love those people. Not because He didn't want them to be able to encounter Him. It was because they had a history of oppressing God's people, leading them astray, and cursing whom God wanted to bless. If such people were allowed to assemble in the temple, it would be even easier for them to lead people away from God. So God restricted their access.

When Nehemiah discovered one such foreigner was given a room in the temple, he threw him out with all his belongings. It seems rude, doesn't it? Not very Christ-like? What we need to understand is Nehemiah wasn't kicking out a person. He was shutting down a foothold. That, my friend, is *extremely* Christ-like. Ephesians 4:27 teaches us Satan can get a foothold in our lives when we sin. If we compromise on what God has said, we authorize Satan to gain access to God's temple. Don't forget: God's temple of today isn't surrounded by Jerusalem's walls. *You* are God's temple! "Don't you realize that your body is the temple of the Holy Spirit, who lives in you and was given to you by God? You do not belong to yourself" (1 Corinthians 6:19).

In your Kingdom work, Satan's unauthorized access to your heart (through anger, bitterness, unforgiveness, etc.) will cause major disruption and damage. If left unchecked, you will become the intruder in God's work! Make David's prayer from Psalm 51:9-10 your own, "Create in me a clean heart, O God. Renew a loyal spirit within me. Do not banish me from your presence, and don't take your Holy Spirit from me."

Credit where it's due (Nehemiah 13:10-14)

The Levites were a tribe of priests whose primary responsibility was to maintain the temple and help the people connect with God. God set up a special system by which the priests would receive a portion of the food. Nehemiah was frustrated to realize that the priests were not being given their wages and portions, and they, along with the temple worship leaders, had to take on other manual labor jobs to survive. More time in the fields meant less time serving in the temple, which meant their tasks were being neglected.

You don't have to work for a church to be considered a priest today. Just as a priest's job is to help people connect with God, isn't your job as a believer to help others (saved or unsaved) connect with God? "You are a chosen people. You are royal priests, a holy nation, God's very own possession. As a result, you can show others the goodness of God, for he called you out of the darkness into his wonderful light" (1 Peter 2:9). Your literal job description is to share God's heart to restore what's broken. That's not a single project or idea, it's a lifelong privilege.

Paul encouraged his apprentice Timothy to make sure those who preached and taught were paid well. "Those who work deserve their pay!" (1 Timothy 5:17-18) It's clear from Scripture that God values His Kingdom workers, and does not expect them to work without compensation, or to take time away from His project to make ends meet.

This matters because too many Kingdom workers burn out due to financial concerns. We can't sit here and tell you what finances will look like in your Kingdom work. We can neither promise a life of poverty nor a six-figure income. All we can do is point you to your true CEO and encourage you to trust that He set up a system to make sure you receive what you need.

Ultimately, give credit where credit is due when it comes to your Kingdom work. It's not shameful to get paid to do the work God has given you if that is a possibility. Don't cut corners when it comes to compensating others who labor with you. *The main consideration here is your heart.* Do you undervalue yourself and your work? Do you make financial decisions about yourself or others based on worry? Are you taking extra, unrelated work because God has truly provided it or because you don't know what to do without it? God's Kingdom economy doesn't look like the world's economy, but He is good and fair and values all who take on the burden of Kingdom work.

Overwork (Nehemiah 13:15-22)

After rebuilding the wall, business in Jerusalem could return to normal—the hustle and bustle in the marketplace, merchants and traders flowing in and out of the shiny new gates. The Jews increased production in the fields and vineyards to keep up with the rising demand of Jerusalem's fertile economy. There was one major problem, however. Time was money, and they were spending more than God permitted them to spend.

You see, long ago, God had established a pattern of six working days followed by one day of rest. Much like today's society, they quickly found reasons to stay busy on that seventh day.

Nehemiah recognized God's people were slipping away from the lifestyle God had originally prescribed for their health, joy, and sustainability. He beseeched the Jews to stop working on the seventh day; he ordered the gates be closed and locked the entire day. When merchants and traders began camping outside the gates, he kicked them out so the Jews inside wouldn't even be able to *think* about the pressures of business.

How's your seventh day? If it doesn't look any different than the other six, it's time to turn it off. Beyond that, maybe you need to close and lock the gates. Restrict access to the places you work. Put the phone away. Close the laptop. Turn off notifications. How's your thought life? Are thoughts of work camping outside your gates? You're not interacting with them, but are you consumed with the thought of them waiting until morning?

"It is useless for you to work so hard from early morning until late at night, anxiously working for food to eat; for God gives rest to his loved ones" (Psalm 127:2).

Overwork is one of the biggest threats to your Kingdom work. Overwork starts with good intentions. You're zealous for the work of the Lord. You don't want to waste any time. You want to be a faithful steward with what God has given you. But over time, your zeal turns to obsession. You start to consider time "yours." Your faithfulness turns to obligation. And eventually, you've taken on all the burdens of Kingdom work onto your own incapable shoulders.

OVERWORK IS ONE OF THE BIGGEST THREATS TO YOUR KINGDOM WORK.

Jesus saw this coming. It's why He invited you long ago to "Come to me, all of you who are weary and carry heavy burdens, and I will give you rest. Take my yoke upon you. Let me teach you, because I am humble and gentle at heart, and you will find rest for your souls. For my yoke is easy to bear, and the burden I give you is light" (Matthew 11:28-30).

Unequally yoked (Nehemiah 13:23-29)

Remember Sanballat? You know, the main villain of this entire story? The one who scoffed, mocked, discouraged, distracted, and attacked Nehemiah throughout the wall-building process? Would you believe one of the grandsons of the high priest ended up *marrying Sanballat's daughter*? What?! Nehemiah couldn't believe it, either! In fact, several other men of Judah had married women from the surrounding pagan nations. Nehemiah confronted them, cursed them, and even pulled out their hair! (v. 25) Okay, that reaction is between Nehemiah and God. We can't in good conscience recommend you pull out someone else's hair, but the truth is, relationships with people who don't submit to God give Satan a foothold in your life. As we talked about earlier, when it comes to footholds, drastic measures may be necessary. It's not a time to be polite.

If you're trying to run the race of Christian living, but you're tied up with someone who has no interest in running, what's more likely: both of you crossing the finish line, or you stumbling and falling in the middle of the road?

Prayerfully and wisely consider who you partner with. Paul warns in 2 Corinthians 6:14-16:

> Don't team up with those who are unbelievers. How can righteousness be a partner with wickedness? How can light live with darkness? What harmony can there be between Christ and the devil? How can a believer be a partner with an unbeliever? And what union can there be between God's temple and idols? For we are the temple of the living God. As God said: "I will live in them and walk among them. I will be their God, and they will be my people."

God has chosen you to represent Him, to live in you, and to walk with you. He wants to be your God, and He wants to brag that you are His. He wants the project He's given you to be a mirror that reflects His light into the world and shows the difference He can make. If you partner with someone who doesn't share this interest, the world around you won't recognize the difference, and they'll continue living in darkness.

The heart of the matter: Consecration

If we were to sum up all of Nehemiah's actions here in these "post-credit scenes," it would be in one word: consecration. It means to protect and separate as holy what God has declared holy. Over time, throughout your Kingdom work, vision slips. Compromises are made. Bitterness sets in. Questionable relationships are formed. Values are forgotten. What started as holy and God-honoring ends up...dusty and inconsequential. It's no coincidence that when it comes to consecration, your next step is provided by Paul, immediately following what we just read about unequal relationships:

"Therefore, come out from among unbelievers, and separate yourselves from them, says the Lord. Don't touch their filthy things, and I will welcome you. And I will be your Father, and you will be my sons and daughters" (2 Corinthians 6:17-18).

Paul isn't saying don't hang out with unbelievers. He's not saying avoid everything that isn't Bible, church, and worship. He's saying you are holy, forgiven, and clean by the blood of Jesus, and don't forget it. If your life doesn't reflect that now, come to Jesus for a reset. He's a good and faithful Father.

In your Kingdom work, you will go through cycles. You will be in seasons of good work and progress. You'll feel light, effective, and productive. You will also be attacked with discouragement, doubt, direct attacks, and distractions. You will need to lean on your community more than once. You'll need to start again, reminding yourself of the problem you see in the world, and falling in love with the people who suffer because of that problem. You'll need to reassess and recalibrate as you study the problem and adjust your plans to help solve it. You'll need to recast your vision for yourself and others. The cycle is not indicative of failure. On the contrary! It is a sure sign you're doing it. You're making progress! Yes, there will be more problems, more people, more challenges, but you're only finding them because you are moving forward. You are different now than when you started.

See Appendix I to take a potentially uncomfortable—but crucial—look at areas in your life where you may have drifted. Be brave; you'll be glad you did!

Our Prayer for You

Nehemiah finished the wall. And we believe if you follow his example and submit your work to Jesus, you will not only start the work that God has put on your heart, you will complete it. What that finish line looks like for you, we don't know. We do know that your story is less about doing that thing on your heart, and more about realizing that *you are the thing on God's heart.*

If you've read all three books in this series, you know the pursuit of God's heart has been central to our entire conversation:

In *The Mountain in the Desert,* we recognized the "wilderness" seasons as invitations from God to know His heart.

In *The Fortress by the River,* we learned God brings us to and through the impossible in order to give us a heart like His.

And now, in *The Rubble and the Wall,* we've shared God's heart for people and taken steps to restore what's broken.

We (Mike and Kelsey) pray for you, dear reader, what Paul wrote to the Colossians, a group of believers he had not yet met, but whose reputation of faithfulness captured his heart:

We always pray for you, and we give thanks to God, the Father of our Lord Jesus Christ. For we have heard of your faith in Christ Jesus and your love for all of God's people, which come from your confident hope of what God has reserved for you in heaven. You have had this expectation ever since you first heard the truth of the Good News. This same Good News that came to you is going out all over the world. It is bearing fruit everywhere by changing lives, just as it changed your lives from the day you first heard and understood the truth about God's wonderful grace.

So we have not stopped praying for you since we first heard about you. We ask God to give you complete knowledge of his will and to give you spiritual wisdom and understanding. Then the way you live will always honor and please the Lord, and your lives will produce every kind of good fruit. All the while, you will grow as you learn to know God better and better.

We also pray that you will be strengthened with all his glorious power so you will have all the endurance and patience you need. May you be filled with joy, always thanking the Father. He has enabled you to share in the inheritance that belongs to his people, who live in the light. For he has rescued us from the kingdom of darkness and transferred us into the Kingdom of his dear Son, who purchased our freedom and forgave our sins (Colossians 1:3-6, 9-14).

We know with all our hearts that you will face impossible challenges as you move forward with what God has put on your heart. The darkness is attacking even now as you set your heart to pursue God's Kingdom. But by standing, reminding yourself, others, and your enemies that you are doing good work and cannot come down, you will see God do more than you could possibly think or imagine. As you grow closer and closer to your Creator and your Savior, your heart will break, and your soul will sing—at times, all of it all at once. God's work in your life produces every kind of good fruit as you get to know Him better and better. But the fruit becomes nourishing only after the tree undergoes pruning, survives long winters and harsh summer heat, and submits itself to growth. Fruit is not easily won, my friend.

When you feel like the work is too much, the road is too long, and you're exhausted, lean into Nehemiah's words as he comforted the people of Jerusalem: "The joy of the Lord is your strength" (Neh. 8:10).

You have a good Father who knows how to care for you. It is for the hope of eternity with Him that we find the courage, endurance, and patience we need to keep going. Don't forget that the Kingdom work you are doing is primarily God's work. Furthermore, you are His work. And what God starts, He finishes.

"He who began a good work in you is faithful to complete it."
Philippians 1:6

Acknowledgements

Just like Nehemiah's project had a community, we have our own people to acknowledge.

Tracy, Leigha, Chelsea, Chris, and Anna, thank you for living your stories and allowing us to share them here. Keep going.

The others in The Grove, whose growth and grit inspired the creation of this book.

Our parents, who raised us to pursue a faith-led life and continue to set that example.

Pastor Rob and our Journey Church family, for your encouragement and for giving us a home to hang our spiritual hat.

Our Adalynne, God granted us profound joy when He gave us you. We love you more than life and are so very proud of who you are.

And above all, Jesus, to think that You would work through us to teach and share Your heart with others is a humbling and astounding experience. We are speechless and grateful.

Appendices A-I

You're here! You found the appendices! Unlike your appendix at the end of your colon, which is forgettable and isn't obviously useful, these appendices greatly increase the value you'll receive from reading this book. These questions are designed to help you reflect on the truths of the Bible, and to equip you to put them into action.

Appendix A

(accompanies Chapter 1)

Before we begin, would you take a moment to answer a couple of questions? They're not for our sake, of course; they are for your clarity to know where you are and where you want to go.

Why did you want to read this book?

Why now? Why not sometime later?

What do you hope to get from this study?

We encourage you to read the book of Nehemiah to serve as the foundation for all the conversations and applications around this book. If you'd rather listen, you can check out Mike's reading of Nehemiah via the Outloud Bible Project Podcast. You can find this wherever you listen to podcasts, or at *outloudbible.com*.

Then, thinking broadly about what you read:

What did you learn or recognize about God through this story?

How is your situation similar to Nehemiah's situation?

What surprised you about Nehemiah's responses and reactions?

Appendix B

(accompanies Chapter 2)

Regardless of whether or not you're an emotional person, there is something in the world you know to be wrong. It shouldn't be this way. People are experiencing pain because of it. And you may not even know what to do about it, but you are burdened by the feeling like you should. Before we can talk about what you're going to do to solve this problem in the world, we need to first clarify what the problem is. Let's start broad and work to narrow it down:

What are three things you see in the world that break your heart?

Choose two that resonate most with you. What do these problems mean for the people involved, who God loves?

Choose one. What would solving the problem mean for their relationship with God?

Once you define the problem, does it rile you up a bit? Does it move you emotionally? If not, try getting more specific. Think of a person who you know to be affected by the problem.

Who do you know who is struggling with this problem?

Appendix C

(accompanies Chapter 3)

R ead Nehemiah's prayer in Neh. 1:5-11. In fact, we encourage you to write it out. Then, write or underline the words and phrases that jumped out at you.

You can form a prayer that is intentional and focused like Nehemiah's prayer. Start by answering these questions:

Who does God say he is?

What mindsets or habits are keeping you from God?

What promises of God from the Bible do you need to lean on more now? (see the next page for a list of many of God's promises)

Complete the sentence: God, I'm willing to...

What tough conversations do you anticipate needing to have in order to move forward?

Appendix C (continued)

(accompanies Chapter 3)

Not sure what God has promised you? Read and consider these promises God has made to all people at all times. *(Note: some are conditional! For example, He doesn't promise to give you peace if you choose to keep worrying. Look for the word "if" to give you a clue about your role in receiving a promise).*

He will never leave you or abandon you (Deuteronomy 31:6, Hebrews 13:5).

He will never stop loving you (Romans 8:38-39).

He is your Helper (Hebrews 13:6).

He will give you wisdom if you ask (James 1:5).

He will instruct and teach you (Psalm 32:8).

He will hear you when you pray (Psalm 34:15).

He will answer when you pray (Matthew 7:7-8).

He will straighten your path if you submit to His lead (Proverbs 3:5-6).

He will forgive your sins if you confess them (1 John 1:9).

Abide in Him, and He will abide in you (John 15:4).

He will give you peace if you take your concerns to Him (Philippians 4:6-7).

Seek the Kingdom first, and He will meet your needs (Matthew 6:33).

The Devil will flee from you if you resist him (James 4:7).

... and more!

Remember, you're not twisting God's arm by quoting back His promises. You're putting your faith in His faithfulness. It's like saying "I know You. I know what You've said. And I trust You."

Now, using your answers to the previous questions based on the format of Nehemiah's prayer, write your own prayer to take the problem to God.

> *Declare who God is.*
> *Confess your sin.*
> *Lean on God's promises.*
> *Offer yourself as a servant.*
> *Ask for favor with others.*

"O Lord, God of heaven...

Appendix D

(accompanies Chapter 4)

Let's practice fighting our urge to find the "best" solution all the time. As quickly as you can, give an answer for each of the following questions:

Give a title for this painting:

Complete this African proverb: "Restless feet might walk you into a…"

Who was the 14th vice-president of the United States?

What ingredients do you need to make a chocolate cake from scratch?

Did you find yourself trying to stop and figure out the "best" answer?

Take a brief break from Nehemiah for a moment and **read James 2:21-24.**

What are you *not* doing because of fear of what will happen, or fear of "getting it wrong"?

Without action, your faith isn't complete. Without faith, your actions are futile. Imperfect action, when prompted by God, is where faith and action meet. You can't run on one without the other.

Read Nehemiah 2:1-8.

Without even visiting Jerusalem, Nehemiah asks the king for three main things to complete the project.

Before we look at them, though, can we notice the fact that he shot up a quick prayer before he asked? Even after all the prayer and fasting leading to this point, he asked God to guide this imperfect, not fully-informed action.

Now's not too early to pray, again, for God to help you take imperfect action.

Write a ten-second prayer asking for God's help.

Now, look at the three requests Nehemiah makes, even before he knew all the information. What imperfect actions can you take in these areas now?

Time (verse 6)

When do you expect to complete your main goal?

Do you need to take time away from other work, projects, or routines?

What changes to your daily or weekly calendar need to be made?

Who could you ask to help you re-prioritize your time?

Protection (verse 7)

What support do you need from others as you go about your work?

Do you need legal backing to do what you need to do?

Who can start this journey with you?

Resources (verse 8)

What does your goal require financially?

What hardware (physical components) could you acquire now?

Who could you ask for some of these resources?

These questions are not meant to overwhelm, but rather to break down your needs into some manageable next steps. You don't need to have it all figured out yet. *But action is better than inaction!*

Appendix E

(accompanies Chapter 5)

At the root of Jeremiah's vision for the future was an admission of the problem. Before you put together a vision statement, take a moment to remember the problem that brought you to this point:

What problem breaks your heart, and you feel called to solve?

With that in mind...
What are you going to do about the problem?

What does "finished" look like?

What will be the result for the people with the problem?

Next, let's put the answers to these three questions together, and form a vision statement. Perhaps this template can work for you:

> **We will ...** [what you are going to do]
> **until ...** [what finished looks like]
> **so that ...** [the result].

How does that sound? Does that pump you up? Tweak some words if you need to. Don't worry about making it "perfect." You're not addressing the United Nations. This can be another "imperfect action."

Write the full statement, and pray over it.

Appendix F

(accompanies Chapter 6)

"And now, dear brothers and sisters, one final thing.
Fix your thoughts on what is true, and honorable, and
right, and pure, and lovely, and admirable. Think
about things that are excellent and worthy of praise."
(Philippians 4:8)

We need a battle plan to combat the discouragements that will inevitably come our way, and prevent them from settling into doubts.

Philippians 4:8 gives us a filter we can use to "fix our thoughts." Take time now to build a defense against discouragements, and then we'll get even more specific.

TRUE

What is true about your project?

HONORABLE

How does your work bring honor to God?

RIGHT

Why is this work the right thing to do?

PURE

What is pure (untouched, intact) about your project?

LOVELY

What is lovely? What do you love about it?

ADMIRABLE

What is admirable about the work you're doing?

EXCELLENT

What is excellent about it?

WORTHY of PRAISE

What about your project are you excited to tell people about?

Note: Apply this throughout your life! Whenever you are faced with worry, negativity, or opposition of any kind, take Philippians 4:8 literally to filter your thoughts. "Is what I'm thinking or hearing true?" "Is it honorable?", etc.

Now, refer to the types of attacks in the "Satan is mean" section of chapter 5.

In that section, we outlined several ways your enemy may attempt to demean you and your work. Raise your sword to parry those strategic discouragements with strategic truths in the questions below. Some questions are specific to you and your work. Some apply universally and are grounded in Scripture.

How valuable are you in God's eyes? (see Matthew 10:29-31, 1 Peter 1:7)

What is true about your strength? (see Psalm 21:7, Psalm 138:3)

What's true about the duration and the goal of this work?

What does "finished" look like?

How is your work an act of faith?

What is the impact this project will have on people?

What does excellence look like for a Kingdom worker? (see Colossians 3:23-24, 2 Peter 1:3)

Appendix G

(accompanies Chapter 7)

Distractions may be the biggest threat to your Kingdom work. They are subtle and finely tuned to the areas of your greatest weaknesses. They aren't even inherently sinful, so they can fly under the radar. Take some time to identify where you are most susceptible.

There's a reason we say "pay" attention. Our attention is a currency, and everything and everyone around us is asking for it. Where are you spending it?

Read C. S. Lewis' quote in the *Opposition #4: Distractions* section of chapter 6 before answering the following questions:

What do you prefer to do over spending time praying? working? sleeping?

What messages, conversations, and content are you "paying" with your attention, through comments, likes, and views?

Time to be brutally honest with yourself. **What "dead fire in a cold room" is neither what you ought to do, nor what you like to do?**

Take five minutes to write **all the things to which you give your attention** in a typical day. Be specific. It doesn't matter if it's positive, negative, small, mundane, or necessary.

Just like a good investor only gives money to the activities that will yield greater value, we need to give our time to the activities that will have the greatest impact in God's eyes.

Think of your list above as your portfolio of current and potential investments.

1. **Draw a checkmark** next to the investments that result in greater value when you pay attention to them.

2. **Draw an "X"** next to the investments that demand more attention than they give back in value.

3. Pray, and then **draw a star** next to the things that are the "best" investments in God's eyes.

Read Colossians 3:2-17. It's time to get serious about setting your mind on things above (verse 2). It's appropriate to take the Bible literally here. Later, in verse 17 (NLT), it says "whatever you do or say, do it as a representative of the Lord Jesus."

How does that command affect how you think about the things you say and do throughout the day?

Your "X" activities (from the previous page) are dangerous distractions. **What are some practical, even drastic, steps you can take to cut off your attention to them?**

Write Nehemiah's response to distractions from Nehemiah 6:3. Use whatever version of the Bible resonates best. Where can you physically place this verse as a reminder throughout your day? When and where are you most susceptible to distractions?

Appendix H

Nehemiah alone was called to do this work, but he was not called to do it alone. He spends several chapters taking inventory of the people around him who contribute at various levels. Consider these areas and prayerfully list those who God brings to mind.

Who are your PARTNERS, who could do the work with you?

Who around you has similar or complementary skills?

Who responded to your vision statement with the most enthusiasm?

Who is suffering from the problem you are trying to solve, and has expressed interest in being part of the solution?

Who are your CHEERLEADERS, the people who are the heart of community and culture?

Who "gets" it?

Who talks about your work to other people?

Who introduces other people to you?

Who is excited about the work?

Who are your MENTORS?

Who are your spiritual mentors?

Who are the leaders who care about your spiritual growth?

Who understands the spiritual nature of the work you're doing?

Who sees this community as an opportunity to grow closer to God?

Who is praying for you?

Who are your RECEIVERS?

Who are the people you know who will benefit most from your work?

Who suffers from the problem you're working to solve, and will finally feel free when it's complete?

Who will occupy the spaces you're creating?

Who are your PREDECESSORS?

Who has come before you to make this work possible?

Who taught you what you know?

List them, pray for them, reach out to them. Share with them the project on your heart, and let them know what they mean to you.

Appendix I

(accompanies Chapter 9)

New problems arise, more imperfect actions are necessary, vision slips, opposition comes from other sources, and your community may change. You may have identified with every step of Nehemiah's story; it doesn't mean you won't have to revisit some steps.

Nehemiah returned to the project, even after it was completed, and addressed new problem areas. Can you identify any of these issues in your life now?

UNAUTHORIZED ACCESS

Read Ephesians 4:17-32, Psalm 51:9-10, and Psalm 139:23-24.

Pray and ask God to search your heart and reveal any footholds Satan has been using in your life to vandalize God's temple (that's you!). **Where have you granted your enemy access?**

CREDIT WHERE IT'S DUE

Do you need to celebrate and compensate someone who is doing the hard work of helping others connect with God? Maybe it's your pastor, mentor, or a co-laborer. Maybe it's you?

On the other side of the topic, are you taking on extra work to pay the bills? If so, was that decision rooted in prayer or fear? (This question isn't to judge, but to do a quick heart check and see if you're aligned with how God wants to provide for you).

OVERWORK

Read Genesis 2:3, Psalm 127:2.

It's easy to forget: God doesn't need you to accomplish His work. Success does not depend on your time and efforts. Rest is not an act of weakness. Rest is an act of faith. Taking a day of rest means you trust God to do more in six days than you can do in seven.

Protect the seventh day. What day of the week will you sacrifice to God to demonstrate your faith in His ability to accomplish His work?

Close the gates. Where does work overlap your personal life? Phone, laptop, books on certain topics, social media? What does "close the gates" look like in your life to protect your rest?

Chase away the merchants. Are you still aware of the opportunities to work, just waiting outside the closed gates? Read Matthew 11:38-30. Ask Jesus to take your burdens and help you be present.

UNEQUALLY YOKED

Consider the people you interact with most, and who have a voice in how you go about your Kingdom work. Partners (in work or in life), clients, bosses, friends, etc.

After reading 2 Corinthians 6:17-18, do you feel like they share your call to become like Jesus and help others do the same?

Pray for wisdom, and talk with 1-2 trusted godly individuals to know how (and if) to proceed with these relationships.

Kingdom Connections

Connect with the people whose stories are shared in this book:

Telling captivating stories rooted in biblical truth
Leigha M Sherman, Illustrator
correlatecomics.com

Empowering women and children
Chelsea Gannon, RISE Women and Children
risewc.com

Uniting the community with hope through music, fellowship, and outreach
Tracy Warren, Revival Day of Hope
revivaldayofhope.com

Restoring people and families to wholeness in Jesus' name
Anna and Chris, Sozo Tanzania
sozo.family

Works Cited

[1] Müller, George. *The Life of Trust: Being a Narrative of the Lord's Dealings with George Müller.* In the public domain, via Project Gutenburg, 115.

[2] Lewis, C. S. *The Screwtape Letters.* HarperOne, April 2015, 59.

About the Authors

Mike and Kelsey have served in creative ministry together since 2009. This has taken various forms. Mike has traveled full-time with *321 Improv* and wrote a book, *Thrown off Script* based on his ex-perience. Kelsey has directed, written, and produced programs and videos for churches across the country. At the core of their work, their desire is to empower Christians understand the Bible and do something about it.

Together, they formed ***Outloud Bible*** (outloudbible.com), where they produce podcasts, study material, and live performances of the Bible so people can hear it, love it, and live it.

They live in New Hampshire with their daughter, Addy, and their bunny, Cinnabun.

HEAR IT. LOVE IT. LIVE IT.

UNFORGETTABLE, ENGAGING
BIBLE READINGS

Ignite hunger for the Word of God
with **powerful and easy-to-understand**
Bible readings for your church or event.

"very moving and **fun**"
- Michael M.

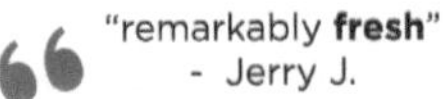

"remarkably **fresh**"
- Jerry J.

"Our church and community
came to see a performance.
They left with a **greater
understanding of Scripture**."
- Rob Willis, Journey Church

20-minute episodes
of engaging reading and application

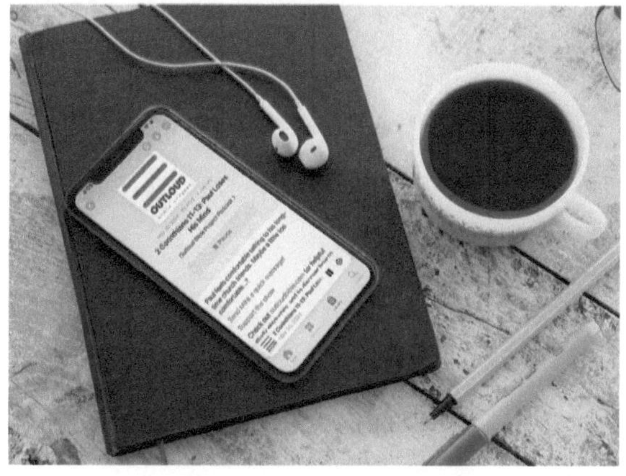

Listen wherever you listen to podcasts

learn more at **outloudbible**.com